"I remember when I was twenty and thinking about all the amazing musicians who come out and do a few great things, and then something happens. It's like they go through a door of success and it changes them. The thing I wondered was whether they just burn out or do they get distracted by the success? My dream was to go through that door and still do interesting things."

BECK

BECK

The Art of Mutation

NEVIN MARTELL

POCKET BOOKS

New York   London   Toronto   Sydney   Singapore

ALSO BY NEVIN MARTELL
Dave Matthews Band: Music for the People

For orders other than by individual consumers, Pocket Books grants a discount on the purchase of **10 or more** copies of single titles for special markets or premium use. For further details, please write to the Vice President of Special Markets, Pocket Books, 1230 Avenue of the Americas, 9th Floor, New York, NY 10020-1586.

For information on how individual consumers can place orders, please write to Mail Order Department, Simon & Schuster, Inc., 100 Front Street, Riverside, NJ 08075.

An *Original* Publication of POCKET BOOKS

 POCKET BOOKS, a division of Simon & Schuster, Inc.
1230 Avenue of the Americas, New York, NY 10020

ISBN: 0-7434-1151-X

First Pocket Books trade paperback printing July 2001

10 9 8 7 6 5 4 3 2 1

POCKET and colophon are registered trademarks of Simon & Schuster, Inc.

Book design by Lindgren/Fuller Design
Title page photo courtesy of Scott Gries/ImageDirect
Cover design by Brigid Pearson
Front cover photo by Niels Van Iperen/Retna

Printed in the U.S.A.

contents

○ Press Play and Sit Back...

eck Hansen is the ultimate example of the postmodern condition. He is a synthesizer of all his scattered musical influences—Hank Williams and Johnny Cash, Woody Guthrie and Ramblin' Jack Elliot, *Spinal Tap* and *American Bandstand,* Leonard Cohen and Rick James, Prince and Devo, Mississippi John Hurt and Leadbelly. This ever-chimerical amalgam is an utterly singular sound maelstrom without boundary or inhibition. Inimitable and forever evolving, Beck may very well be popular music's brightest sonic asset and greatest hope for the future.

After honing his songwriting skills on the New York antifolk scene in the late eighties and releasing several indie slabs, Beck finally struck gold in 1993 when his imminently catchy single "Loser" became an omnipresent anthem for the generation that has been dubbed merely "X." In a time of Seattle grunge and East Coast/West Coast rap rivalries, the single scored a #1 hit on the *Billboard* charts and went gold. But despite a multiplatinum debut, *Mellow Gold* drew equal amounts of acclaim and disdain from the popular media. Not too many people were betting that the quirky Cali boy was anything more than a flash in the pop cult pan. However, once he'd delivered the praise-showered *Odelay,* which gave rise to such hip-shakin' genre benders as "Where It's At," "Devils Haircut," and "The New Pollution," the pundits shut up.

Beck's 1999 offering, *Mutations,* harkened back to his acoustic roots, proving his viability and range as a performer and songwriter. Then, amid plastic boy bands and rap metal meatheads, Beck dropped *Midnite Vultures,* a millennial pièce de résistance that skates from one influence to another, while remaining grounded in a nouveau appreciation of old school R&B and white boy soul. This quartet of major label offerings is just the tip of the iceberg. One of the most prolific, diverse, and studious songwriters of the past decade, Beck is in an endless conversation with the cosmic muse.

Intentionally alienating himself from "the norm," Beck operates as the outside insider in today's music industry establishment. *The Art of Mutation* is a journey to Beck's world within our wider world where the only constant things are change and zealous experimentation. This is the story of a stylish tastemaker, a revolutionary musician, a spirited performer, and an incomparable force in contemporary pop music. This is the story of Beck.

CHAPTER 1

Even in His Youth

"I didn't have that social know-how, I didn't have those cliques. I was on ... my own island. ... It really liberated me to just form my own universe, really form my own view of the world. I wasn't influenced by what all the other kids did. I was able to step back from the culture at the time."

The man we know today as simply Beck was born in Los Angeles at 11:59 P.M. on July 8, 1970, as Bek David Campbell. His parents, David Campbell and Bibbe Hansen, were an artistically inclined couple who would prove to be a considerable influence on Beck's art. He was the younger of two; and his brother, Channing, would follow his own creative path over the years.

Born and raised in the Great White North of Canada, David Campbell grew up the son of a preacher man. His father, a Presbyterian minister, filled the young lad's head with classical and choral music from the get-go, and Campbell's future began taking root. At the age of nine, he moved down to Seattle where he began taking violin lessons. At one point, he performed with David Harrington in a string quartet (Harrington would later go on to lead the critically acclaimed Kronos Quartet). In the mid-sixties, Campbell relocated to

New York to study at the Manhattan School of Music. After this burst of formal education, the young Campbell switched coasts to L.A. to pursue a career in music. It was there he began to appreciate the pop maestros of the time, falling in love with the Beatles, the Rolling Stones, and Leonard Cohen.

Campbell's big break came when he was chosen to back Jackson Browne on the viola for "Song for Adam," a tune that ended up on Browne's massively popular eponymous debut. Soon thereafter, he hit the road with Carole King's traveling band, an opportunity which led to him arranging strings on King's *Rhymes and Reasons* album. This record plucked Campbell out of virtual obscurity when it peaked at #2 on the *Billboard* charts, while the single "Been to Canaan" hit the Top 25. This résumé builder was the cornerstone of his professional career, and he ultimately went on to become one of the music industry's most called-upon studio musicians and string arrangers. He has contributed his skills to over eighty gold and/or platinum albums for artists as diverse as Joe Cocker, Leonard Cohen, Green Day, Neil Diamond, R.E.M., Dolly Parton, Alanis Morissette, Linda Ronstadt, and Aerosmith, while playing on such timeless slices of pop memorabilia as Marvin Gaye's "Let's Get It On" and Bill Withers's "Lean on Me." Beck says that his father "always had an ear for the weirder harmonies. That's probably what he passed to me."[1]

Beck's mother Bibbe is an equally compelling artist. Born in New York, she was Warhol's youngest star when her fifteen minutes started at the tender age of thirteen. She starred in Warhol's unreleased 1965 film *Prison* opposite Edie Sedgwick, as well as in a production for avant-garde filmmaker Jonas Mekas. After a chance trip to L.A., she moved out West and continued to be a part of the art scene—acting in B movies, founding a theater company, rocking out with the gender-bending band Black Fag, and serving as a documenter of the area punk-rock scene. When she married Campbell, the couple moved to Hollywood, where she soon gave birth to Beck (then Bek).

It may have been Al Hansen, Bibbe's father and Beck's grandfather, who had the most influence on Beck. He was most likely the family member from whom Beck learned the most, as well as the artist who most inspired Beck's later work. A native of Queens, New York, Hansen was an avid fan of

2

drawing and sketching from an early age. Due to World War II, he wasn't able to follow his artistic muse throughout his early adulthood, and instead joined the air force. While stationed in Frankfurt, Germany, he pushed a grand piano off the top of a bombed-out five-storey building and listened to its cacophonous crash. This explosion of noise was a life-defining moment for him, and it would later serve as the impetus for his performance-art piece "The Yoko Ono Piano Drop," in which he would push a piano from a great height.

Upon his return Stateside, he studied at New York's Art Students College League, Brooklyn College, and the New School for Social Research, where he met his mentor John Cage. Hansen later wrote, "One of the things John Cage taught was, that if you began to compose music, or paint, or make a dance and you knew what the end product would be, then you were not experimenting. To experiment one sets out to do things without knowing what the end result will be. You must agree in advance. John always said to accept whatever happens. So the end product is a 'happening.' This is exactly the way I did all my Happenings. Free form. No rehearsals."[2]

Hansen became heavily involved in the Happenings scene and in 1965 wrote *A Primer of Happenings and Time/Space Art,* which came to be widely regarded as a must-have tome in artistic circles. The gifted avant-garder was a part of Warhol's Factory; in fact he was one of the first people to discover the injured pop artist after SCUM (Society for Cutting Up Men) leader Valerie Solanas shot him (Hansen bumped into her in the elevator as she made her hasty retreat, smoking gun still in hand). He later made a book about the incident entitled *Why Shoot Andy Warhol?* In another *Pop-Up Video* aside, Hansen is even responsible for Velvet Underground's moniker: "It was a few weeks before their first gig, and they were calling themselves Falling Spikes or something and desperately looking for a better name," Beck remembers. "Al had this semipornographic book called *The Velvet Underground,* and he was having lunch with their manager one day, and he said, 'Well, this is a good name. Why don't you use it?' The manager ended up taking credit for the whole thing and said it was *his* book."[3]

Along with his Happenings, Al was closely associated with Fluxus, an art movement of the late sixties and early seventies that challenged conventions with playful games, odd performances, and a willingness to push all boundaries. In his own essay on the matter, Al describes a movement that is founded in its lack of structure or definition: "Anyone who thinks Fluxus is serious misses the point. One who thinks Fluxus is not serious is closer to the point, but still misses the point. A unique thing about Fluxus is it is also not 'in-between.' Fluxus is not between 'this' and 'that.' Fluxus is everywhere at once. And nowhere. Its secret is—it does not really exist—but it exists. In that way Fluxus is like God—it might not exist. But we talk about God and we talk about Fluxus." Or, as Ben "Obi-Wan" Kenobi once intoned, "The Force is what gives a Jedi his power. It's an energy field created by all living things. It surrounds us and penetrates us. It binds the galaxy together." The movement's critical players included George Maciunas, Ben Vautier, George Brecht, Robert Watts, Allison Knowles, and even John Lennon and Yoko Ono, who became close friends of Hansen. In 1970, the trio collaborated on a piece entitled *This Is Not Here Show* in Syracuse, New York. Despite all this, Hansen may have garnered the most public attention for his collage work, in which he created a variety of Venus figures out of Hershey wrappers, cigarette butts, lighters, or whatever found detritus he could incorporate.

Beck was probably most literally influenced by Al's *Intermedia Poems,* in which the poet would take random headlines and put them together to form collagist poems. A sample of one piece steals poetry from the headlines: "The rooster, the hawk and the phoenix/The McMiracle Continues: A Cool Head Wins a Heated Crapshoot/Bills Find New Way to Pain Raiders: The Boot in Overtime/Monetary milestone on a European two-speed road to ruin." Beck would later mimic the form in his own lyrics—the opening lines of "Loser" read like an Intermedia Poem; "In the time of chimpanzees I was a monkey/Butane in my veins so I'm out to cut the junkie."

These three figures in Beck's early life brought an incredible amount of creative and artistic energy to bear on his childhood circumstances. There was always something different going on in the household when Beck was growing up. "There was definitely an environment where it was cool to sort of do your own thing and be interested in whatever," Beck said.[4] As involved as his parents were in his well-being, Beck's mother had a very hands-off approach, "I take no credit for Beck's creativity—he came into the world with it, and I recognized early on that he was gifted. But I did create a similar environment for him."[5] "I guess you'd call it an artistic home," Beck offered. "It wasn't like *You Can't Take It With You,* where people were sliding down the banisters doing ballet and somebody was down in the basement inventing something. But if you showed up with weird hair or did something funny with clothes, it wouldn't be out of place."[6]

It was only in retrospect that Beck realized what a privileged childhood he had had from an artistic standpoint. "Some people would put a lot of value into certain family customs, like a yearly picnic or Bar Mitzvah. With my family, it was a Truffaut movie or some art object by Joseph Beuys—things which I certainly took for granted. The more I talk to other people about their backgrounds, the more I realized I had a whole other experience."[7]

Growing up, Beck was always a prolific and dedicated artist. Long-time family friend Brendan Mullen remembers, "Bibbe told me that when Beck was nine years old he started making his own cassette albums out of found sound, poetry, writing, and banging on the guitar. He'd come home after school and go into his room, which he kept very neat, and just write, write, write. He was dedicated to being an artist at a very young age, and when he was still a child, told his mother, 'This is what I want to do for the rest of my life.'"[8] To prove his commitment to his vocation of choice, Beck produced a small literary and art magazine called *Youthless* that he circulated amongst friends and family. His grandfather didn't ignore this interest and enlisted the aspiring artist to scour Sunset Boulevard for cigarette butts for one of his endless stream of projects when he was in town. Al even went as far as to fly Beck to Cologne, Germany, several times for visits and impromptu tutoring while he worked on founding his own art institution, the Ultimate Akademie. Beck's brother, Channing, began to take an interest in their grandfather's work as well, and would go on to become a second generation Fluxus artist.

Beck's parents split up when he was nine, leaving the youngster to spend his childhood shuttling between two very different worlds—Kansas City, where he lived with his father's father, the Presbyterian minister; and his mother's home in Los Angeles. His name had changed from the irregularly spelled Bek to Beck because grade school teachers continually misspelled it, and he chose to keep his mother's maiden name after the divorce. Beck lived most of his younger life up in Hollywood Hills, but then his mother decided to make the move down to the lower class area around 10th and Hoover upon her divorce. This meant a change of districts down to the less-than-desirable Belmont High School, which was the first high school to actually have airport security detectors installed at the doors. Years later he half-joked, "I'm sure there's something good about high school, but not any of the ones I went to."9 So, before even starting the 9th grade, Beck dropped out.

"The year I was supposed to start high school I tried to get into the High School for the Performing Arts, which had just opened. I sent them a tape of me playing blues guitar and some short stories I'd written, but they didn't want me."10 Undaunted, the fifteen-year-old pursued his growing love of music on a personal level. After hearing the blues at a friend's house one day, Beck stole his unopened copy of a Mississippi John Hurt album and his fate was sealed. "It was shrink-wrapped, it hadn't even been opened, and it was this insane close-up of his face, sweating, this old, wrinkled face, and I took it. I was going to return it, but I didn't. I loved the droning sound, the open tunings, the spare, beat-down tone. And his voice was so full. He just went through so much shit, and it comes across really, really amazing."11 Beck nearly wore the vinyl out, listening to it over and over. Before long, he picked up the guitar and started tracing the blues family tree. Records by Mance Lipscomb, Blind Willie McTell, Robert Johnson, Leadbelly, Son House, and the slide blues of Blind Willie Johnson all found themselves on the spindle in Beck's room. An accidentally discovered Woody Guthrie LP infected him with the folk bug as he continued his self-taught guitar tutorings.

Beck's record collection was at odds with both the popular music of the time and his neighborhood. "I grew up in a Salvadoran ghetto. Me and my brother and mother were the only white people in the area. I don't come from a privileged background. I didn't relate to the shiny eighties bands like INXS and Huey Lewis and the News. I grew up hearing ranchero music and hip-hop.... It's not like I'm usurping this stuff because it's suddenly cool—I've just gone where gravity has pulled me musically."[12]

His predominantly Latino neighborhood acted as a veritable melting pot of sounds and stylings. His bus rides turned into mini–music education classes; "...there'd be some kids in the back who got on way down on Vermont in South Central. And they'd have their boom box blasting [Grandmaster Flash's] 'The Message.' Then, coming up through Wilshire, some white girls would get on. Then, you get up to Hollywood and some freaks would get on. And soon everybody on the bus would be singing the lines, doing the moves. It was great."[13]

Despite the intriguing variety of characters and influences growing up, Beck was somewhat at odds with his surroundings and socializing. "I grew up hating [L.A.]. Sometimes it has this feeling of a deserted place; there's millions and millions of people but they are all in their cars and houses.... As an adult, I came to realize it was a part of me. If you hate it, you end up hating a part of yourself. So eventually I was reconciled with the fact that this is me whether I like it or not."[14] He was a self-described loner: "I didn't have that social know-how, I didn't have those cliques. I was on...my own island.... It really liberated me to just form my own universe, really form my own view of the world. I wasn't influenced by what all the other kids did. I was able to step back from the culture at the time."[15]

Without a prototypical family or schooling situation, Beck was mostly left to fend for himself when it came to education, entertainment, even cooking. This unorthodox but artistically appreciative environment, combined with his strong personal will, was the perfect situation for the young artist. Indeed, it was probably Beck's alienation from, yet close observance of, popular culture that was the largest philosophical stepping stone in his evolution as an artist.

The Gonzo Years

"I started pushing from the beginning. I was playing folk songs like they were punk rock songs. Like, I'd play a Woody Guthrie song, but it would have some Black Flag in there too. I'm sure that's the way Woody Guthrie would have done it today."

After spending several years bumming around L.A. and working on his chops whenever possible, the young Beck decided he needed a change of pace and scenery. In 1989, he hopped a bus with his girlfriend and headed cross-country. "I began to feel like there was nothing going on for me in L.A., so I took the bus to New York. Maybe it was all those years of reading Kerouac and Bukowski, or the stories of my grandfather, or being descended from nomads, but I wanted to get out there and see what was going on."[16] Upon their arrival, the nineteen-year-old aspiring musician was acrimoniously dumped by his girlfriend and left drifting amid Gotham's urban sprawl. Instead of attempting to find a home of his own, he skated from couch to couch and claimed sleeping space in whatever squatter's quarters he could find, while doing everything from ID photography at a YMCA to coat checking at a bookstore in order to make some spare change.

In a case of accidental timing and sheer luck, there was a musical phenom afoot that would help guide Beck toward his eventual success. The East Village was vibrating with the underground "antifolk" scene. This neofolk movement was a radical deconstruction of the traditional folk that had dominated the Village in the sixties and seventies, and served as the antithesis to Pete Seeger and Woody Guthrie's All-American Left-Wing Folk-Song Revival of the forties.

"It was just a very aggressive kind of folk played with punk energy, punk-rock energy," Beck said. "It wasn't as simple as that, you know, it's not that easily summed up. But it was a lot of people just being free with what they were doing, and nobody had anything but an acoustic guitar."[17] "The whole mission was to destroy all the cliches and make up some new ones."[18] Indeed, the entire scene was ruled by its unpredictable nihilism, "There was this whole kinda punk rock folk scene and noise-music-chaos-poetry-underground-basement-40-ounce-malt-liquor-being-crazy scene going on."[19]

Though antifolkists drew influence from the classic folk movement, this new generation of artists was intent on deconstructing and reforming its values and methods. As a songwriter and performer, Beck never expressed his influences in a straightforward manner or adhered strictly to their original qualities. "I started pushing from the beginning. I was playing folk songs like they were punk rock songs. Like, I'd play a Woody Guthrie song, but it would have some Black Flag in there too. I'm sure that's the way Woody Guthrie would have done it today."[20] The burgeoning movement in general found fertile inspiration in Bob Dylan's early music, though Beck largely eschewed the elder statesman's work. "I never really identified with him as a person...his art and music, they're undeniable, but...I'm probably more influenced by Leonard Cohen and Ramblin' Jack Elliott and other folk people than Dylan. I guess to me he is so realized in himself, he's a cul-de-sac.... He did what he did and achieved what he did so fully...there's no real point to retread it."[21]

In his first hesitant steps as a performer, Beck casually booked gigs and showed up for open-mic nights, sticking to what he knew best, covering Woody Guthrie and Mississippi John Hurt. Clubs like the Fort at Sidewalk Cafe, Chameleon, ABC No Rio, and casual late night jams at Tompkins Square Park were aiding the festering scene of which Beck yearned to be a part. However, he didn't really have any original material to contribute at the time. "I hadn't really written a song to speak of, just fooling around. And I was trying to get a gig at this place and was playing into an open mic, and this cat, Latch, said he wouldn't give me a gig until I wrote some songs. So I went and wrote some songs. It was the same twenty or thirty people, so once they had already heard a song once or twice, you had to write a new one. So there was a high, high turnover, a high volume of songs going on. So I had a lot of years where I was writing a lot of songs. Everybody was writing songs, everybody was influenced by each other's songs, and those people were breaking into rap stuff, and hip-hop was coming in, all kinds of things."[22] As with Fluxus, there was a desire to ignore convention, embrace the spontaneous, and dig into the proverbial melting pot of inspiration whenever possible. "You could go up onstage and say anything, and you wouldn't feel weird or feel any pressure,"[23] he recalled several years later.

Strumming a battered Silvertone acoustic and sometimes wearing a *Star Wars* Stormtrooper mask, Beck began to amass a collection of compositions. Pulling lyrical influence from every part of the cosmic fabric he could get his hands on, he would strap those lines onto whatever melody floated out of his guitar. Beck spoke to *BAM* magazine with his usual flair for odd metaphors when describing his songwriting process: "I open up a big cabinet, and I have a collection of helmets. I put on the different helmets, and I take three bottles of Robitussin and drink them really quickly. Then I set my hands on fire—I have to write down whatever comes to mind pretty fast, before my hand burns off."[24] "I just let whatever comes out, come out without thinking about it too much. Some of it I keep, some I toss out, some of it I turn into giant cigarettes and smoke 'em. I think everybody should just turn off their TV machines and make up their own songs about whatever comes to mind—their couch, their friends, their loaves of bread. Everybody's got their own songs. There should be so many songs out there that it all turns into one big sound and we can put the whole thing into a pickup truck and let it roll off the edge of the Grand Canyon."[25] When asked for advice on how to write a song using the Beck method, he joked, "Set your guitars and banjos on fire and before you write a song, smoke a pack of whiskey and it'll all take care of itself."[26]

The antifolk scene was led by such characters as Michelle Shocked, King Missile's John Hall, Kirk Kelley, Roger Manning, Billy Syndrome, Paleface, and Cindy Lee Berryhill. Beck ended up befriending Manning, who in turn watched the West Coaster transform himself. The first time he saw Beck play, "It was like seeing the ghost of Woody Guthrie,"[27] Manning remembered. That's a powerful image to associate with a fledgling singer/songwriter, but Beck would go on to transcend even Manning's great expectations.

Eventually Beck started committing some of his newfound compositions to tape, usually on 4-tracks in bathroom-cum-recording studios. After accumulating a bevy of tunes, he put out a homemade cassette, *The Banjo Story,* which contains very early versions of "Let's Go Moon Some Cars" and "Goin' Nowhere Fast." To make a little extra cash, he would sell copies on the street for three dollars a pop. Another interesting rarity from this period is a tape entitled *Fresh Meat + Old Slabs,* a collection of roughly recorded tunes that Beck gave his mom for her birthday. This unofficial outing includes the first airings of later Beck favorites such as "Fume," "Satan Gave Me a Taco," "Tasergun," and "Steve Threw Up." Though it's nearly impossible to find original copies of either tape, both have been pressed up by bootleggers, and these bootlegs are relatively easy to locate. Various "definitive" versions of both bootlegs include a slew of additional demos and unreleased tunes from this period.

Despite Beck's involvement in the budding antifolk scene, he gravitated back to the West Coast in 1991. When talking to his hometown paper several years later, he said that New York was "a much more complicated and expensive place...a harder place in general to live."[28] Back at home, the shiftless strummer began working a series of McJobs, and his résumé read like a scene from *Reality Bites*—he painted signs, worked in a video store, and had a stint as a leaf blower, a job he joking still holds sacred: "There's a leaf-blower contingent [in L.A.]. There's no union that I know of so far, but there's certainly a spiritual brotherhood. They are the originators of noise music. It's like a cross between a Kramer guitar and a jet pack."[29]

Beck makes extra cash playing the wedding circuit. PHOTO COURTESY OF FRANCIE SOOSMAN

It was anything to make ends meet, as long as he could still make music. In these early days, he could be found playing at Onyx, Raji's, Al's Bar, or any party that had space for a lone performer. When he had no set venue, he would play the part of the busker on street corners or in the backs of buses, anywhere that wouldn't boot his earnest performances. These solo sets weren't his only musical outlet—he would jam with his friend Steve Hanft's punk-metal act, Loser. Their live show featured a coffin out of which Beck would emerge playing screamin' metal-guitar leads. It was that sarcastic po-mo 'tude that would later help define the Beck vibe and look. Always trying to outdo himself as a performer, Beck would randomly set his guitar on fire to pique the jaded interest of Los Angeles hipsters.

As his skill and repertoire expanded, his gig regimen picked up playing the Silverlake coffee shop scene alongside bands like Ethyl Meatplow and that dog. Otherwise, as Hanft recalled, "Beck was just living in this shed behind someone's house, recording his weird surrealist folk songs on a 4-track."[30] According to Hanft, he lived on watermelon, wore found clothes, and, though it wasn't the case at all, would insist on telling people, "I only listen to Slayer."

Living in L.A. and being around an entirely different music scene began to morph his palette of influence. After falling in love with the suavely debonair James Bond flicks, he picked up a Pussy Galore record and found their messy brand of accidental noise sonically immaculate. Jon Spencer and company's production aesthetic served as a great influence on the way Beck was recording his own compositions. The crude "multitrack" demos he made around this period often consisted of him recording himself playing live, while playing back the sounds from another take to create layers of resonating back-wash.

In early 1993, the tiny indie label Sonic Enemy gave Beck the chance to release his first official album, *Golden Feelings*. Seventeen tracks long and limited to one thousand cassette copies, the majority of these tunes were 4-tracked in whatever bedroom or basement Beck was crashing in when the muse struck him. Opening with "The Fucked Up Blues" and continuing through "People Gettin Busy," the collection stands as a vague promise of things to come and an important document in Beck's evolution as a songwriter and performer. Interestingly, *Golden Feelings* marks the first semiofficial collaboration between Beck and Steve Hanft, who can be heard mumbling semi-incoherently at the beginning of "Heartland Feelings": "I'm totally fucked up. I can barely speak. I'm totally fucked up. They gave me so many drugs."

The first thousand copies sold quickly, so Sonic Enemy pressed several additional runs until 1995. However, after Beck left the label's roster and his career shot skyward, the album was rereleased once more. The Sonic Enemy Web site now bears the following humorous quip to the frequently asked question, "Hey, where's Beck?": "Beck doesn't live here anymore. Mommy says the mean lawyer people took him away to live with his other family, even though he lived with us first. Mommy says I'll understand someday." Despite being "officially" unavailable, bootleg copies are still obtainable for the dogged collector.

It wouldn't be *Golden Feelings* that broke Beck, though. The story of Beck as a force in pop culture begins at a street fair on Sunset Boulevard, where Bong Load Custom Records co-owner Rob Schnapf saw Beck performing. Impressed by Beck's presence and setlist of original material, Rob told the other half of the label, Tom Rothrock, about his new discovery. A week later, Tom caught Beck's impromptu set at a Jabberjaw show where he performed "Cut in Half Blues" from *Fresh Meat + Old Slabs* and a couple other ditties during a set break. Despite not knowing that this was the same performer his partner had mentioned the week prior, Tom chased down Beck after the show to see if he'd be interested in putting anything to tape, and Beck agreed. Later that night, Tom and Rob compared notes and realized they both had been overwhelmed by the same artist.

Only five days later, Tom and Beck went over to producer Karl Stephenson's house to play around. Beck laid down some slide guitar, Stephenson looped it, and then Beck freestyled over a Public Enemy-esque beat. When he found himself at a loss for words when the chorus came around, he came up with a chant meant to criticize his own performance — "Soy un perdedor," which means "I'm a loser" in Spanish. Unbeknown to any of the three at that moment, the appropriated phrase would soon enter into the American Mexi-lexicon along with other noteworthy South-of-the-Border phrases as *Ay caramba; Hasta la vista, baby;* and *Yo quiero Taco Bell.* Beck's impromptu rapping also spawned the now-classic addition to the Beck patois, "Get crazy with the Cheeze Whiz."

"When we recorded 'Loser,' that was the first time I ever rapped," Beck admitted. "The chorus should have been, 'I can't rap worth shit.'"[31] The threesome then added a sample of Dr. John's "I Walk on Gilded Splinters" (a cover of which Oasis would later sample for their single "Go Let It Out") to Beck's spoken-word spoutings and cut in some choice soundbites from the imminently quotable President George Bush. "Loser" was complete. Sometimes indecipherable, definitely ironic, and infinitely catchy, this shoddily tracked tune was about to set an unstoppable ball in motion.

Before anyone heard "Loser," however, Beck released a very limited edition split vinyl 45 in 1993 with the band Bean (whom he had played with briefly) via Gusto Productions/Flipside Records on clear blue vinyl (later reissues of the single are on clear or black vinyl). Beck contributed "To See That Woman of Mine" and the satirically titled "MTV Makes Me Want to Smoke Crack," while Bean added "Privates on Parade" and "Rock > Scissors > Paper" on the B-side. The version of "MTV Makes Me Want to Smoke Crack" on this 7-incher differs greatly from the lounge take found on Geffen's "Loser" CD EP the following year. On this original version Beck sarcastically croons, "I watch those videos, I watch 'em all day/And I plug 'em in my eyeballs hey yah/And the colors are nice, and the pictures are nice/And the girls are nice, everything's so nice."

Beck stopped jabbing his finger at the man to return to his living room recording sessions and amass more material. On January 11, 1993, Beck officially signed to Bong Load Custom Records; and in May of '93, "Loser" backed with "Steal My Body Home" was pressed up as a limited edition 12 incher on Rob and Tom's fledgling label. The B-side is a minilament that Beck had solely penned, while songwriting credit to the A-side is split between Beck and Stephenson. Recording credit for the pair of tunes goes to both Stephenson and Rothrock.

This one small slice of black vinyl was the beginning of the end of Beck's incognito status. At first the single only received airplay on indie and college stations, but then some big-time commercial stations started playing bootlegged tapes of the song. Two of L.A.'s finest, KXLU and KCRW, started spinning the tune, and the world began hearing the phenomenon known as Beck. From L.A. the word spread, and soon tastemaker DJs everywhere were covertly slipping the song into their playlists. Indeed, when the song was added at Seattle's influential KNND six months later, it quickly became the station's most requested song over Pearl Jam's "Daughter," no small feat for an indie artist going up against a major label act with millions of dollars of marketing behind it.

"I can remember the exact moment when I realized my life was about to change," Beck said. "It was in August of 1993. I hadn't released an album yet, but 'Loser' was a hit on the radio. I was on a bill with four other bands for a Sunday concert, and I spotted a girl in the audience who was about fourteen years old and had my name written on her forehead in Magic Marker. It absolutely terrified me, and I don't know why. Maybe if I'd been a little older or was in a band with some friends, I would've enjoyed that moment, but for me, it all happened so fast and so awkwardly."[32]

With DJs nationwide making a name for him, there was suddenly a lot of attention directed at Beck and his artistic output. The artist himself wasn't taking any notice, though, letting Schnapf handle most of the press inquiries, booking requests, and business calls. He did grant a few radio interviews, performed on both KXLU and KCRW, and played some low-profile area gigs. But for the most part, Beck was trying to come up with a cohesive album of work to deliver to Bong Load. Talking to *Rolling Stone* about recording during that period, Beck remembered: "[Karl's] girlfriend would come home and make food after work, so I'd be hurrying up to finish a vocal before she came in."[33] It was rough 'n' tumble times with every possible expense being spared. Popular rumor has it that the entirety of the album was recorded for a mere three hundred dollars.

During a recording break, Beck recorded "Steve Threw Up" with his friends, producer Tom Grimley, and some members of that dog, at Grimley's Poop Alley recording studio. The title is a reference to Tom Moramarco of Bean, though the exact inspiration for the song's story is unknown. Bong Load actually released the tune, backed with "Mutherfuker" and a short untitled piece from the Tom Rothrock and Karl Stephenson sessions, as a follow-up 7-inch to the "Loser" single; but it was destined to be overshadowed by Beck's debut, *Mellow Gold.*

In the end, a total of twelve tracks made *Mellow Gold,* as well as an unlisted bonus track of random aural detritus. The final listing was "Loser," "Pay No Mind (Snoozer)," "Fuckin' With My Head (Mountain Dew Rock)," "Whiskey-clone, Hotel City 1997," "Soul Suckin Jerk," "Truckdrivin Neighbors Downstairs

(Yellow Sweat)," "Sweet Sunshine," "Beercan," "Steal My Body Home," "Nitemare Hippy Girl," "Mutherfuker," and "Blackhole." Beck had considered titling the album *Cold Ass Fashion,* but changed it to the backhanded pot reference *Mellow Gold,* which name-checks a particularly enlightening Cali strain. Production credit of the project goes to Beck, Tom Rothrock, Rob Schnapf, and Karl Stephenson, with mixing going to the two Bong Load men. Songwriting credit is given solely to Beck with the exception of "Loser," "Soul Suckin Jerk," "Sweet Sunshine," and "Beercan," which are cocredited to Stephenson.

Playing the album through, one is greeted with a variety of styles, production aesthetics, and moods. *Mellow Gold* is a send-up to all of Beck's scattered influences with a flare for not taking itself too seriously. Despite the seemingly frivolous and irreverent air of the collection, Beck was making a serious artistic statement with his debut—sometimes that which seems the most obvious is indeed the most complex and difficult to truly comprehend. Coming in as track number two after the pop bombast of "Loser," "Pay No Mind (Snoozer)" is a simple guitar dirge complemented with a keening harmonica solo that sounds inspired by a late night on the prairie huddled around the campfire. At the beginning of the track, a voice can be heard chirping like a stoned chipmunk on nitrous: "This is song two on the album. This is the album right here. Burn the album." Beck then launches into some of the best lyrics on *Mellow Gold,* including the priceless couplet, "Give the finger/To the rock 'n' roll singer." Talking about the origins of the song and its sarcastic wordplay several years later, Beck remembers: "That was me, nineteen years old, enjoying writing songs for the first time...when you start writing songs you're so in love with the idea that anything—that Dixie cup—that's a song!"[34]

"Fuckin' With My Head (Mountain Dew Rock)" is a fuzzed-out slice of mid-sixties San Fran psychedelica, while "Whiskeyclone, Hotel City 1997" is a listless low-key acoustic affair. The lyrics for "Soul Suckin Jerk" disregard the classic folk tradition as they paint a fractured picture of his minimum wage years: "I got a job making money for the man/Throwing chicken in the bucket with the soda pop can/Puke green uniform on my back /I had to set it on fire in a vat of chicken fat."

The antifolky rant "Truckdrivin Neighbors Downstairs (Yellow Sweat)" starts out with a supposedly real taped argument involving Beck's neighbors, including the odd taunt, "Come on motherfucker, put your clothes on!" Urban legend maintains that one of his neighbors was missing an arm from a drunken argument that ended when one roommate took an axe to the other in a moment of rage. Beck's description of his building mates is as venomous as it is droll: "Whiskey-stained buck-toothed backwoods creep/Grizzly bear motherfucker never goes to sleep."

Paying tribute to his lo-fi foundations, "Sweet Sunshine" sounds like Morphine experimenting inside an acid-filled aquarium. Beck's distorted vocals are laid over a sludgy bed of rhythms with an occasional minimalist choir and space-age samples. In direct contrast, "Beercan" has a bouncy loop with a muted bassline that borders on a dancehall mentality. At one point he cops a line from Kool Moe Dee, "How ya like me now?" before laying down this vision: "I quit my job blowing leaves/Telephone bills up my sleeves." The song hints at his R&B leanings as he faux-sleazily proffers lines like "Just shake your boots and let it all get loose" and "Oh yeah/I like it like that."

The sweet requiem "Steal My Body Home" is chorus-less and relentless as Beck moans "Watch my troubles all unwind/Drinkin' gasoline and wine" against a spare drumbeat peppered with Indian strings, a plucky guitar riff, and, of all things, a kazoo solo. Another man-and-his-guitar song, "Nitemare Hippy Girl" is musically in the same vein as "Pay No Mind," with a slightly more upbeat bent. The lyrics are shot with a heavy dose of sarcasm as Beck depicts a laughable tie-dyed sixties wannabe: "Yo, she's busting out onto the scene/With nightmare bogus poetry."

Barely two minutes in length, "Mutherfuker" bludgeons on with little subtlety and raw production. Definitely the throwaway track on the disc, it originally appeared as "Mutherfukka" on *Golden Feelings*. The album's track-listing closes with the Zeppelin-esque lo-fi of "Blackhole," the only song of the dozen that mimics the morose, minor-chord grunge of the time. With bass courtesy of Possum Dixon's Rob Zabrecky and violin by that dog's Petra Haden, the tune sounds as if it might be a Chris Cornell side project or a cast-

off from Alice in Chains' *Sap* EP. After a couple minutes of s
tweaky sonic tomfoolery greets you with a crash of Ga
synth craziness, and other knob-twiddling delights. Ther(
madness, it's just a burp of creativity to close out the album.

What Beck had in his hands at the end of his recording sessions was
a zeitgeist-seizing slice of pop postmodernism. It was mindful of the past
while brazenly irreverent of tradition, sarcastic and ironic as it was soulful and
insightful. It was erratic and it was cohesive. It could mean everything or it
could mean nothing. It would become a truly classic album of its time.

Turning *Gold* into Platinum

"Irony is a part of life, it's a modern vessel of expression, but it's not the be-all and end-all. It's easy to hide behind, and it has become symptomatic of a time, at least in America, where people are afraid to stand up and take a chance, do something foolish, say what they feel."

Mellow Gold was now finished, but Bong Load didn't have a major-label distributor for their independent release. This was much needed, since a major could relieve the financial and promotional strain on their struggling indie operation. Rob and Tom felt they had a hit record on their hands and wanted to give it the most exposure possible. The process to find a big-label home would prove easy—the overnight success of "Loser" had not been overlooked by the music industry machine in L.A.; and the burgeoning singer/songwriter was being feverishly courted by labels, managers, and publishers. One-time manager John Silva remembers, "I went to see him at Raji's maybe two or three weeks after getting a tape of 'Loser,' and I was so excited. I remember coming home and my wife asking what I thought. I told her, 'I don't know what this guy is doing, but he's doing something important.'"[35] Silva would soon come onboard as Beck's manager, adding him to an impressive roster that included alternative mainstays like Nirvana and the Beastie Boys. Right after this was decided, Beck signed a publishing deal with BMG Songs, Inc., choosing Cyanide Breathmint Music to be his publishing cognomen.

Popular myth holds that over ten labels swooned for Beck's signature, including Capitol and Warner Bros., but Beck spent nine months turning down the major labels when they first approached him, "'Cause I didn't want to be in that world. It's like you lose control. And as soon as you're on that level, you're immediately, it's perceived that you're asserting yourself as some kind of like, 'I'm the greatest, I'm a rock star.'"[36]

Geffen Records eventually won the gig after intense negotiations. At the time, David Geffen's label was one of the most powerful bastions of alternative rock. Their extensive roster boasted the likes of Nirvana, Sonic Youth, Hole, Weezer, Counting Crows and the Sundays. And so, on November 19, 1993, Bong Load entered into a third-party deal with Geffen to distribute Beck. It was a revolutionary contract for artistic control that allowed Beck to record for any independent labels he chose, as well as the major-label monolith. As Geffen A&R representative Mark Kates said, "We signed Beck for who he is and that includes being an artist who wants to continue to do his various independent projects. In our view, it's all just part of his creative process and it would be a waste of time to try and change him."[37] Kates later continued in a separate interview: "A lot of people think that it's sign of weakness when an artist is constantly going in different directions—and it is, if you don't do them well, but one of Beck's strengths is his extraordinary range and depth."[38]

Discussing this unique deal years after joining forces with a major label, Beck admitted that the music industry didn't appeal to him unless it was on his terms: "I was pretty aware of the music industry treadmill, the revolving door. I've been playing music for a lot of years, so I was always very reticent about having some business people dictate to me what I should be doing. It seemed way too foreign to me. I always did music for my own amusement, which is how anybody starts playing music.... It's easy to be seduced by all that stuff. But I didn't start writing music because I wanted money or needed to be successful. But the thing with 'Loser,' it sort of took on a life of its own and was a hit before I was on a record label. So I was lucky in having some leverage. It's pretty rare that a song comes out of nowhere."[39] It was a position that very few performers are ever fortunate enough to be in. Whereas most artists have to prove their "commercial viability" over the course of their first album or two, Beck had already proven it through a grassroots radio success. Geffen knew they were guaranteed at least one runaway hit, so to them it was a surefire moneymaker no matter how the legalese finished up.

"They just took the song and ran with it, and I'm like, 'Yoo-hoo, I'm back here.' I didn't get that much money," Beck says about the deal he eventually signed with Geffen. "I got enough to pay my rent for a year and buy some equipment and stuff. But it wasn't a money deal. If I'd wanted to get a lot of money, I could've gotten three times as much."[40]

Strong believers of the carpe diem mentality, Geffen chose to release the already red-hot single before the album hit shops. They hastily serviced an official radio cut of "Loser" to stations nationwide and pressed up an EP in time for the holidays. The five-song disc afforded the purchaser four unreleased bonus tunes from the various unused recording sessions, "Corvette Bummer," "Alcohol," "Soul Suckin Jerk (reject)," and "Fume," which has a particularly interesting story behind it. "These two kids kickin' in the Valley somewhere and they had a can of nitrous, but these guys got inspired," Beck told a L.A. radio station. "They were in this pickup truck and they rolled up the windows and said 'How 'bout we just fill up the whole cab with the nitrous?' And so they did that and it killed 'em. I guess they got really high. So I kinda got inspired, like, what they saw just before death. They were so high, y'know? They were just at that peak of nitrous, that kind of nirvana, whatever."[41] In other nitrous-related news, the album art for *Mellow Gold* featured a sculpture by Beck's friend Eddie entitled *Last Man After Nuclear War,* which borrowed most of its knobs, widgets, and doodles from a nitrous inhaler and is topped off with a strange prehistoric skull.

Not wanting to waste any more time, Geffen asked Beck to speedily shoot a video for "Loser," so Beck turned to his longtime friend and filmmaker Steve Hanft. A multitalented visual visionary, Hanft's video résumé now includes the Cure's "Gone," a pair of Primal Scream clips, the Jon Spencer Blues Explosion's "Dang," and Luna's svelte swoon of a song, "China Town." His films include a number of shorts, the 1998 Elliott Smith documentary *Strange Parallel,* and *Kill the Moonlight* (parts of which you can see in the "Loser" vid if you keep your eyes peeled). In a flashy collage of scenarios throughout the "Loser" video, fans can see Beck play acoustic guitar in a headdress, wash car windows, use the leaf blower on the crowd (footage Hanft captured at Raji's back in 1993), and jump, jive 'n' wail in a suit that a seventies pimp wouldn't be caught dead wearing. Oh, and then there is the prerequisite "cheerleaders-dancing-in-the-graveyard" routine. The blur over Beck's face at the beginning of the clip covers a Stormtrooper mask. Despite Beck's obvious love for the white-suited goons of *Star Wars,* the homage had to be removed due to some "official displeasure" with its use from the folks at Skywalker Ranch.

As the single, video, and EP caught fire with consumers, prerelease demand was at a fever pitch. Even though Geffen was rushing to release it to radio, many radio stations had already been spinning bootleg copies of the song just so they could add it to playlists and sate listener demand. On Christmas 1993, "Loser" entered the *Billboard* Modern Rock Tracks chart at #25. It quickly ascended to the #1 position on February 5, where it remained for five weeks straight. It peaked on the Hot 100 Singles Airplay chart at #31 and on the *Billboard* Hot 100 at #10, selling over half-a-million copies. "Loser" is the only song from an indie label that has achieved Top 10 chart status on *Billboard* since the birth of FM radio. Beck's pastiche of references, ad-libs, and broken slogans had undeniably connected with the Generation X crowd.

Not only were they connecting with his lyrics, but people were diggin' on Beck's style—a laid-back fusion of fashions that found him in a "Bob's Burrito Barn" T-shirt and a pair of corduroy pants one moment and a cowboy shirt and trucker-styled baseball hat the next. His lanky frame seemed to be shrugging off whatever he was wearing, leaving him looking poised on dishevelment and casual disarray. The media quickly attached this look to what they had surmised was Beck's "slacker" lifestyle and soon enough Beck had unwittingly begun a mini–fashion movement which manifested itself in malls and high-school halls across America.

Time proclaimed that "Loser" "has become an anthem of nihilism chic among slackers."[42] In fact, many took the song to be exactly what it was not—a glorification of tuning in, turning on, and dropping out to embrace a devil-may-care lifestyle. Even when the runaway hit was at its peak, Beck was uncomfortable with the popular media's assertions that he was the spokesman for the slacker generation. In many ways, "Loser" had become a parody of its intention. He defensively told *SPIN,* "I've always tried to get money to eat and pay my rent and shit, and it's always been real hard for me. I've never had the time or money to slack."[43] He reiterated that stance with his usual stoned abandon to an L.A. radio station, "I don't know what's up with slackers. That's for rich people. I never had time to be a slacker. I'm trying to get some beans for a burrito." Beck was frustrated with the public's misconception of the song's intentions: "Irony is a part of life, it's a modern vessel of expression, but it's not the be-all and end-all. It's easy to hide behind, and it has become symptomatic of a time, at least in America, where people are afraid to stand up and take a chance, do something foolish, say what they feel."[44]

The catchy teen anthem wasn't just a Stateside sensation. Overseas, especially in Europe, Japan, and Australia, the song was making serious inroads with pop culture connoisseurs. On February 24, 1994, Beck made his first appearance on Britain's *Top of the Pops* alongside the fey Suede, the tantra-trained Sting, pop maestro Bryan Adams, and Tommy Mottola's latest conquest, Mariah Carey. "It was like being in the Doors or something," Beck recalls, "because they had these big psychedelic lights in the back swirling around 'n' stuff. And there was all these fourteen-year-old skinhead kids jumping up and down and going 'Ho, baby, ho.' "[45]

For the next six months, Beck and "Loser" were ubiquitous no matter where in the world you were. "Weird Al" Yankovic later made reference to the song in his anti-alt rant "Alternative Polka," and the harmonica-totin' hippies in Blues Traveler tossed a cover of it into their setlist on occasion. Indeed, from talk-show hosts to stand-up comics, everyone was making references to the tune for months thereafter.

With a #1 single suddenly to his credit, Beck was instantaneously a name on the lips of everyone everywhere, though it was never part of his own masterplan to become famous. "I never really wanted to draw

Beck meets with Jimmy the Idiot Boy and his mentor. PHOTO COURTESY OF SCOTT J. HURTWITZ, 2001

attention to myself. I was just going to do my thing and play for friends of mine and make up songs about people that we knew and make up jokes that only my friends could understand."[46] "I remember when I was twenty and thinking about all the amazing musicians who come out and do a few great things, and then something happens. It's like they go through a door of success and it changes them. The thing I wondered was whether they just burn out, or do they get distracted by the success? My dream was to go through that door and still do interesting things."[47] The astounding success of "Loser" had changed Beck's life forever and had given him a fresh platform by which to address the world at large, though he would have to continually prove and reprove his desire and ability to "do interesting things."

This newfound success continued to boggle the mind of the still-struggling artist. "All the shit that's happening to me now is totally insane, because if you ask anybody that knows me, they'd tell you I've had the worst fucking luck. This is all an avalanche of confetti and balloons and kazoos. Before, the party was just an empty room with a bare lightbulb on the ceiling. It was pretty bleak."[48] There would be no more bare lightbulbs and empty rooms. From this point on, Beck would always draw a crowd no matter where he went.

As the single continued to explode, Geffen quickly pressed up copies of *Mellow Gold* and released it on March 1, 1994. The album entered the *Billboard* Top 200 at #15 to begin a twenty-four-week run. Though the album would peak at only #13, *Mellow Gold* was nonetheless a bona fide smash. Despite the public and the media's misinterpretation of "Loser," the album was generally embraced by music critics. Robert Christgau wrote a very positive snapshot review of *Mellow Gold* alongside Pavement's *Crooked Rain, Crooked Rain* in *Playboy:* "Rock and roll fosters idealistic fools who believe they create the world anew. But at its root, this music is more derivative than other arts and crafts—especially since the advent of the rap sample. These days, there are young wiseasses who borrow known stuff, treat it as if it belongs to them and mean to make you love it. On *Crooked Rain, Crooked Rain* and *Mellow Gold,* Pavement and Beck exploit this process as sarcastically, gleefully and impressively as any newcomers in memory."[49] The review ends on this high note: "These records won't just be noticed. They'll be remembered."[50] *Rolling Stone*'s Michael Azerrad added, "Beck makes ultrasurreal hip-hop-folk that harkens back to 'Subterranean Homesick Blues'...Beck's verbal collages get close to the truth of his milieu and our times. Think of it as generational code or stream of unconsciousness. But it's really called poetry."[51]

With records moving out the door like hotcakes, Geffen decided it was now time to take the show on the road. The first formal tour for the newly crowned star began inauspiciously at the Goat's Head club in Houston, Texas, on March 20 and lasted until the end of April. Employing local musician-freaks from the L.A. scene as his backing band, Beck concentrated on the East and West Coast markets, bringing a slew of *Mellow Gold* tunes but also dotting his set with older songs and unreleased compositions like "Jimmy Carter" and "Teenage Wastebasket." After taking a five-week breather, he toured the midlands and hinterlands of America, blundering and reorganizing his way through his limited repertoire. One particularly disturbing scene happened at Austin's music conference South by Southwest in 1994. "I was playing to a tape machine and the band started doing free-jazz shit over it, and I was screaming into this cheap mic. I broke a bunch of stuff and started humping

Shades of Kurt. PHOTO COURTESY OF FRANK MICELOTTA/IMAGEDIRECT

the bass player and knocked my mic over and hit this poor girl in the head. I remember watching the room just clear out."[52] Beck wasn't used to playing with a band—much less to large crowds—and his inexperience was clearly evident.

Despite people's misgivings about Beck as a viable live force, "Loser" and the folks at MTV had become best buds. The video had been elevated to the coveted Buzz Clip status, with Beck's upbeat slapstick poetry striking a refreshing chord between overly self-serious grunge lyrics and violence-laced rap wordplay. In direct reaction to the Nirvanabees of the world, Beck wrote "Bogusflow," which appears on *DGC Rarities Vol. 1.* Supposedly a pisstake of "Even Flow" by Pearl Jam, the only public offering of enlightenment from Beck about this song are his cryptic liner notes: "Pulling up roots . . . again. Stranded in the decaying harbor. Surfing in the oil spillage." A lo-fi folky strum accompanies Beck's strained voice (which sounds like it has taken one too many hits from the gravity bong before the recording session) as he pokes fun at the overly earnest blue-eyed grunge of Eddie Vedder, "California white boy sound/Rocket-powered and nailed to the ground."

Indie-pop icon and cultural critic Momus pontificated on the power of Beck in the times of "Smells Like Teen Spirit," 2Pac, and *Singles.* "Grunge had one answer for a decade in which rock and pop got all corporate and shiny and hyped-up sounding. And it was this fierce white Nietzschean noise rock. Death, guns, heroin, pain, machismo. Beck had another answer. He brought back the folk meme. But it was a mutant folk, a folk that acknowledged the impossibility of definitive origins, a fragmented and fake folk. Electronic folk, handmade in lo-fi home studios by media savvy Gen Xers sick of shiny corporate pabulum."[53]

The public was obviously yearning for this new sound Beck had created. Three months after its release on May 3, *Mellow Gold* hit the gold standard, having sold more than half-a-million copies in the United States. Geffen offices around the world were calling on Beck to tour their territories to support promotion of the album overseas. So, to keep American fans busy when he departed on his foreign travels, "Beercan" was released as *Mellow Gold*'s second single on July 16. It peaked a week later at #27 on *Billboard's* Modern Rock Tracks. The dancey tune with its funky bassline was seen as a somewhat disconcerting contrast to the hip-hoppish bombast of "Loser" and never achieved the same notoriety. Once again, the fine folks at Geffen pressed up a new piece of product in the form of a goody-filled EP for fans that included "Got No Mind" (an alternate version of "Pay No Mind"), "Spanking Room," "Asskizz Powergrudge (Payback '94)," "Totally Confused" (from the 10-inch *A Western Harvest Field by Moonlight),* and an unlisted Muzak-ed version of "Loser." Well worth the cash output.

Despite the fact that everyone wanted a piece of Beck, he turned to Steve Hanft again for video direction. Hanft had been granted an enormous amount of leeway when making the "Loser" clip; and, since no one at the label seemed to truly grasp the "alternative" movement, he was granted even more freedom for the "Beercan" vid. There's a performance sequence this time, with Beck and bandmates ripping it up in a living room somewhere with a rainbow banner in the background. Buzz Osborne of the Melvins and Vaginal Crème Davis of Black Fag fulfill the "celebrity cameos" quotient as strange homeless men run amok. There's also a very Devo-esque moment as a fully costumed Beck makes funky-funky with the synthesizers—a referential motif that would be later repeated in the vid for "The New Pollution." The clip got more than a few spins on MTV's *Alternative Nation* and *120 Minutes,* helping solidify Beck's media presence at the time.

While "Beercan" was making inroads on radio playlists and MTV at home, Beck embarked on a ten-date Australian tour, then headed on to New Zealand, China, and eight stops in Japan during August and September. Foreign audiences loved Beck wholeheartedly—his music, attitude, and persona were such a contrast to what else was emerging from the States at that time. As Momus commented: "He was the first American artist to be as alienated from the traditions of American pop music as British and Japanese artists had always been. And that alienation is really important, because when all music is a kind of junk store you can pillage freely from, and when you dispense with stereotypes of naturalness and appropriateness (white male artists should rock; females can only be singer songwriters; the French can only do variete; Brazilians, bossa nova; etc.), you're suddenly in a realm of intoxicating freedom and dizzying possibility. You're at the gates of the Kingdom of the Fake."[54]

Foreign fans really connected with Beck's allegiance to the global mindset that borrowed heavily from a variety of flavors and influences that had no borders. His swift intellect and ability to wield sarcasm and irony were more suited to a European rocker than an American alterna-pop star, while his music was as nationally uncategorizable as it was universally attractive. "I've always felt a little distant from American culture," Beck admitted. "Because, speaking in broad terms, things that truly capture the American ideal are usually pretty one-dimensional. I don't want to say 'lowest common denominator' because I'm not snooty about it, but maybe there's not much room for ambiguity. You're really only allowed to be one thing here, so when I came out it was, 'You are the slacker, that's your thing.' That's great, but can't I be a couple of other things? And I think if you want to achieve true success here you have to say, 'OK, that's all I am.' You have to be that cartoon forever."[55]

When the journalist followed up by asking, "Surely what makes you truly un-American is the irony in what you do?" Beck replied, "Yeah, I'd say there is a fair amount of irony here, but there wasn't for a long time. Canadians have it—with someone like Leonard Cohen there's irony. You'll be in the middle of the most heavy Leonard Cohen song and he'll just say something so funny and ridiculous, like . . . erm."[56]

Despite his growing worldwide popularity, Beck was called back to the land of Stars 'n' Stripes for an eleven-date East Coast tour in the fall of '94. After that, the powers that be shuttled him across the Atlantic for his first proper European tour in November. Here he expanded his fan base as quizzical Europeans finally got to see the sensation in the flesh. Beck crisscrossed the continent, hitting France, Spain, Italy, Denmark, Germany, the Netherlands, Sweden, England, and Belgium, taking time out of his busy schedule to make a cameo as a gold panner in the Steve Hanft-directed clip for the Stone Roses comeback single, "Love Spreads."

The final single culled from *Mellow Gold* was "Pay No Mind." Once again, Beck turned to Steve Hanft to achieve the visuals, and once again Hanft delivered a perplexing mishmash of imagery. Bathed in green light and wearing a homemade "Rock Me" shirt, Beck is caught strumming a pawnshop acoustic in a forest setting before we are catapulted off to shots of erupting lava, rotating diamonds, skateboarders, and a surreal cocktail lounge. To publicize the release, he stopped by MTV's *120 Minutes* to jam out with Beastie Boy Mike D and labelmate Thurston Moore of Sonic Youth on some almost unlistenable noise before taking a moment for himself and performing a solo acoustic rendition of "Pay No Mind."

The tumultuous year rounded out with Beck playing a pair of high-profile California gigs, one at L.A.'s famous Troubadour and one at San Fran's Slim's. It had been three hundred and sixty-five strange days for the singer/songwriter, as he was propelled from obscurity into the blinding light of pop-culture stardom. *Mellow Gold* was a resounding winner on the critics' lists that year, cementing some credibility to his sales figures and endless MTV exposure. The album was *SPIN's* #2 album (behind Hole's *Live Through This),* and the rag showered additional love by splitting their #1 "Single of the Year" award between "Loser" and "Beercan." Elsewhere it landed at #10 on *The Village Voice's* "Pazz & Jop Critics Poll" and #31 on *NME's* "Top 50."

However, the biggest critical surprise came in early January when it was announced that "Loser" had been nominated for a Best Male Rock Vocal Performance Grammy. Though it would go on to lose to Tom Petty's "You Don't Know How It Feels," this nod from such a prestigious body in the music-industry machine boded well for Beck's continued support from Geffen.

Aside from a couple of one-off gigs, Beck spent the winter and spring of 1995 off the road and recuperating from his sudden change in lifestyle. He was booked for Lollapalooza that upcoming summer, and there were other facets of his life that required attention. Still surprised by his meteoric career path, the young artist was completely unused to having any kind of extra cash and a guaranteed place to crash, so the time off allowed him to adjust to his newfound living situation.

I'm a Lollapaloozer, baby, so why don't you kill me?

However, the retreat from the public eye couldn't last forever and, as a warm-up for the Lollapalooza shows, Beck did a five-date California mini-tour. On the second night of the outing, June 21, 1995, Al Hansen passed away in Cologne, Germany. It was a great loss for Beck, his family, friends, and the artistic community as a whole. In the days that followed, Beck wrote a eulogy to commemorate his grandfather entitled "Masai Ticket for Al." The demise of Al must have been very hard on Beck, who looked to him as a beloved family member, an artist, and an inspiration. He was gone but not forgotten.

Despite his loss, Beck finished up the tour and after less than a two-week break was back out on the road. Lollapalooza 1995, Version 5.0, featured Pavement, Cypress Hill, Sonic Youth, Hole, and the Jesus Lizard. Despite the credibility factors dripping off the bill, Perry Farrell's traveling rodeo faced poor ticket sales without a truly dazzling headliner to entice crowds. Oftentimes Beck would do a solo acoustic set on the second stage after doing his mainstage gig as a way to keep his old-school folk chops up to par. As he wryly joked, his memory of the tour is less than glamorous: "What comes to mind? Oh, blue plastic seats. Empty. Very empty. And it's 105 degrees, and there's a small cluster of youngsters who are displaying their energetic support, but they're about a mile and a half away, and there's ten security guys closing in on them. I think at that point there was a lot more happening at the falafel booth than where I was standing. It was a good experience because the other bands were really bored, too. We played a lot of ping pong."[57]

Already sick of drunken fratboys with pierced nipples and NC Game-cocks calling for his signature hit, Beck started substituting "I'm a softie, baby, so why don't you squeeze me" in the "Loser" chorus. As the song became an albatross around the young artist's neck, one can imagine Beck wondering whether that one misunderstood moment would be the only moment people would remember him for. To further liven up his sets and keep it interesting for himself, Beck varied his setlist to include some pre-*Mellow Gold* tunes and some new unheard material. Despite his misgivings,

Beck conjures the folk muse. PHOTO COURTESY OF FRANK MICELOTTA/IMAGEDIRECT

fueled mostly by the record company's insistence that he go out and promote product, Beck plugged away show after show. The effort didn't go unrewarded, and on August 8, 1995, *Mellow Gold* went platinum, commemorating sales of one million copies.

At the end of this seemingly endless summer, he hit the European festival circuit and then the land "Down Under" at the end of December. U.S. Beck fans seeking a constant flow of new material during his overseas touring were well-sated during this period of his career. Over the course of 1994, surrounding the release of *Mellow Gold,* Beck also released three independent albums: *A Western Harvest Field by Moonlight, One Foot in the Grave,* and *Stereopathetic Soul Manure.* The first, *A Western Harvest Field by Moonlight,* came out in January of 1994 in a limited edition run of 3,000 10-inchers on Fingerpaint Records. Each original pressing came with a fingerpainting that Beck and his friends had done at the record release party for the set. The dozen-song collection includes hard-to-find fanatic pleasers like "Totally Confused," and "Gettin Home," as well as some of Beck's more garishly titled ditties like "Mango Vader Rocks!," "Feel Like a Piece of Shit (Crossover Potential)," and "Styrofoam Chicken (Quality Time)." Poorly recorded and roughly wrought, the collection serves as an enlightening demonstration of Beck's transient evolution as a songwriter.

Additionally released prior to *Mellow Gold* on February 22, 1994, *Stereopathetic Soul Manure* arrived via Gusto Productions/Flipside Records. The twenty-three-track collection is a variety of material recorded between 1988 and 1993 and demonstrates Beck's noisier, more experimental side. Sounding like a soulmate of Captain Beefheart's misunderstood avant-garde masterpiece *Trout Mask Replica,* the collection highlights Beck's mercurial ability to write and play whatever style strikes his fancy. One standout player on several tracks is steel guitarist Leo LeBlanc, who has gigged with John Prine, Jerry Jeff Walker, and the Wallflowers. The only previously heard tune in the collection is "No Money No Honey," which Beck had originally released on 1993's *Golden Feelings.* Despite very little promotion, the collection has sold over a hundred thousand copies.

To round out the threesome, *One Foot in the Grave* was released on June 27, 1994, through K Records. The set was actually recorded right after the *Mellow Gold* sessions in October of 1993 and January of 1994 by producer Calvin Johnson. Johnson multitasks as a part-time Beat Happening member, K Records founder, cofounder of the Halo Benders (along with Built to Spill's Doug Martsch), and as an acclaimed producer. The list of musical contributors to the sessions reads like an indie rock wet dream: Chris Ballew (Presidents of the United States of America) on bass and guitar, James Bertram (Lync, 764-HERO) playing bass, Sam Jayne (Love as Laughter, Lync) lending some vox, and Scott Plouf (the Spinanes) on drums. Beck handled vocals, guitar, drums, and bass during the recording sessions.

This primarily acoustic album was recorded at the Dub Narcotic studios in the rainy Pacific Northwest and serves as an unofficial tribute to bluesman Sonny Terry, the blind harmonica legend who continues to be remembered for his work with guitarists Brownie McGhee and Blind Boy Fuller. A vibrant part of the forties folk scene in New York City, Terry rose to fame alongside Beck's heroes Leadbelly and Woody Guthrie. *One Foot in the Grave* is a rough-and-tumble album that hints at Beck's ability to blend jagged layers of sometimes atonal sound over a gorgeous pop hook. Notable tracks include the chipper opener "He's a Mighty Good Leader" and the bluesy pluck of "Hollow Log." In addition to this full-lengther, K Records released a 7-inch in 1995 that included three outtakes from these sessions: "It's All In Your Mind," "Feather In Your Cap," and "Whiskey Can Can."

Patrick Maley shot an ultra-lo-fi low-budget clip in grainy black-and-white with color footage flickering in and out to accompany *One Foot in the Grave*'s lone single, "Forcefield," which helped the album sell over a hundred and forty thousand copies. In one scene, Beck takes his own cue and gives the camera the finger, proudly wearing his Stormtrooper helmet (which he didn't have to blur out this time for some reason). In another scene, he plays a retro-hip garage sale gunslinger replete with plastic pistols and a quick draw. At different points throughout the clip, random words appear on the screen like bits of Al's poetry. One sequence reads "Smoke. Ramen. Toast." Better advice is hard to find.

This trio of albums was an important set of releases for Beck. They established his indie credibility during a time when some pundits were loudly questioning both his artistic integrity and musical ability. Despite the cries of detractors, it had been another banner year—larger tours, more videos, higher record sales, and increased media attention. However, performing and promoting had become increasingly frustrating for the highly prolific and deeply motivated artist. Due in part from pressure from the label and the lack of time to write new songs, Beck had been playing the same songs for two years now, though his neofolk instinct was to constantly pitch new material at his audience. No matter that *Mellow Gold* had been a critical and commercial success—Beck didn't want to be filed away in the rock 'n' roll history books as a one-hitter who got lucky. The only thing that could prevent this fate would be a mind-boggling sophomore major-label effort that exceeded everyone's expectations—most of all his own.

CHAPTER 4

Beck to the Future

"Rock 'n' roll, know what I'm saying?/Everywhere I look there's a devil in waiting."

Going into the sessions for the second album, there was an incredible push from the label to follow-up the success of *Mellow Gold* and "Loser." *Billboard* asked him about that pressure to replicate his initial success. Beck could only say, "The world of radio is a very separate world. It's a very finite, narrow, spectrum. That's the way it works, and it works for them, and I guess it works for other people. The best I can do is put music out there, and people are going to grab onto it, or they're not. I have already way surpassed my expectation about getting my music out there, so I'm already way ahead. The 'could have been' or 'would have been' doesn't exist for me."[58]

Speaking later on the same issue, the frustrated songwriter admitted, "I think that song ["Loser"], that whole album got taken out of context. I got portrayed a lot as a clown. I take what I do very seriously.... I place more emphasis on the music and the songs than on the image. I don't really play the star pedestal game. There are situations where the fact is, your video is on MTV and that's a reality. When the whole 'Loser' thing, the slacker thing was happening, I knew it would go away. I just wanted to concentrate on my music. I always feel a need to go to the next place."[59] It was this need to move on, to confound the critics, and to overwhelm his fans, that festered inside him as he contemplated and created his next move.

At first, Beck intended to record his sophomore effort for Geffen with Rob Schnapf and Tom Rothrock at the helm in the fall of 1994. Originally planned as a somewhat stripped-down, mainly acoustic offering, Beck scrapped the concept after completing almost an album's worth of material. There was a feeling the latest songs didn't represent enough of a drastic evolution of Beck's ability. Beck was insistent that whatever his second major label effort was to be, it was going to destroy expectations and set a new standard.

With the original sessions discarded and both labels biting their nails, Beck turned to John King and Mike Simpson, known collectively as the Dust Brothers to coproduce and cowrite his sophomore album. The brothers Dust met in 1983, spinning shows at Pomona College's radio station. Soon they were DJing parties, but it wasn't until 1989, when they signed a production deal with Delicious Vinyl, that things really started taking a turn for the better. The pair produced Tone-Lōc's classic ode to the ladies, "Wild Thing," and other seminal hits on the label before helming the Beastie Boys's genre-crackin' *Paul's Boutique*. The groundbreaking album is considered revolutionary within production circles for its use of digital sampling within the context of rap. With this supreme accomplishment under their belts, the much-sought-after pair went on to work with a broad range of acts, including Hanson, White Zombie, Shonen Knife, the Rolling Stones, Korn, Filter, and A Tribe Called Quest.

Like *Paul's Boutique,* the amount of sampling done during Beck's new recording sessions was staggering—almost every track is littered with slivers of another musician's work. One notable sample that didn't make the final cut was Cell Phone Barbie squeaking, "Come to my house Tuesday for pizza." When Mattel threatened to sue him for everything, Beck let it drop from the curriculum. Beck and the Dust Brothers's penchant for long-forgotten blips on the musical map is evident throughout the list of contributors, as they borrowed everything from Moog meanderings to soul revues.

The majority of the writing and recording of what would soon become *Odelay* was done at the Dust Brothers's house in the Silverlake region, affectionately referred to as PCP Labs. More than thirty tracks were laid down over the coming months, with Beck and the Dust Brothers splitting production, writing, and mixing credit almost entirely. The twisted lovechild of these three men was, for the most part, written as it was played. "There's often a lot of chaos in the studio," Beck admits. "I'm sure when I mix things together there is a certain amount of chance involved that leads you to a somewhat final place where it all sticks together. But there is that tightrope-act aspect to the whole process. And it's interesting to work with this in the context of the music business. . . . I tend to go in [to the studio] and pick up one instrument at random, see what happens, and go from there. I'll build it putting things end to end and over one another. I haven't formulated any tried and true process. It's definitely the mood. There are times when you struggle and have to get it together, and then there are times where everything flows, where there's a magic to it and you don't have to think about it."[60] Beck himself played more than a dozen instruments on the album, toying with a variety of guitars as well as flitting off to play drums, bass, and even clarinet. Additional musicians were only called into the sessions when a part seemed too daunting.

For the entire recording process, Beck immersed himself in the creation, spending hours upon hours in the studio experimenting with various ideas and tasting different avenues. He basically cut himself off from the rest of the world, mostly seeing just his close friends, his girlfriend Leigh Limon, the Dust Brothers, and whatever musicians were wandering in and out.

Finally, after close to a year of studio sessions, the album was complete. The opening number, "Devils Haircut" (originally titled "Electric Music for the Summer People"), is held together with a pair of samples — "Out of Sight," written by James Brown and performed by Them, Bernard "Pretty" Purdie's "Soul Drums," and elements from "I Can Only Give You Everything," written by Philip Coulter and Thomas Scott. Beginning with a rolling guitar riff and quickly breaking into a funky beat companioned with a fuzzy bassline, its idiosyncratic take on what is considered danceable makes its hook all the more beguiling. The lyrics are classic freestyle Beck, though one couplet, "Rock 'n' roll, know what I'm saying?/Everywhere I look there's a devil in waiting," seems to speak of Beck's innate distrust of the music industry. Despite the interpretation, producer Mike Simpson openly admits, "I don't know what he's saying. It's like haiku."[61]

The eclectic Hansen seemed to be digging "Pretty" Purdie around the time of making *Odelay*, because he also cops a sample from his ditty "Song for Aretha" for the tune "Hotwax." He couples this with a clip of "Up on the Hill" by Monk Higgins and the Specialties, giving it a beat that slinks along like a drunken barrio cowboy at high noon. Beck reverts back to the Mexi-lexicon for the chorus, chanting "Yo soy un disco quebrado/Yo tengo chicle en cerebro," which translates to "I'm a broken record/I have bubblegum in my brain."

Beck gets sole writing credit for "Lord Only Knows," which has an opening scream courtesy of a quick sample of Mike Millius's "Lookout for Lucy." Like the prior track, there's a twang and drawl to Beck's delivery, fading out on the confounding couplet, "Goin' back to Houston, do the hot dog dance/Goin' back to Houston, to get me some pants." Opening with the catchiest set of "do-do-do"'s since the late fifties, "The New Pollution" begins with a melodic shuffle and quickly brings it up to a break-dancing shakedown. Powered by a whip-crack beat, a swirling sax solo, and a sample of Joe Thomas's "Venus," it would become one of Beck's biggest singles ever.

"Derelict" is one of only four songs on *Odelay* that doesn't contain a sample. Perhaps the most simplistically structured song on the album, "Derelict" was probably written when an acoustically minded follow-up was in the cards. The next song on *Odelay* was provisionally titled "Novacane Expressway" during the 1995 Lollapalooza tour, but was later shortened to simply "Novacane." Lyrically, Beck takes the listener on a helter-skelter, amphetamine-tinged road trip that brings together Hunter S. Thompson's brutally acidic imagery and Oliver Stone's twisted cinematic vision: "Blowin' static on the paranoid shortwave/ Short fuse, got to dismantle."

Borrowing a clip from Bob Dylan's "It's All Over Now, Baby Blue" as performed by Manfred Mann, "Jack-Ass" is perhaps the most straightforward

At the Y-100 Festival in 1999. PHOTO COURTESY OF SCOTT GRIES/IMAGEDIRECT

pop song in the collection. Lacking the typical verse-chorus-verse structure, the tune nonetheless possesses the poignant simplicity that only three chords and the truth can convey. Listening back a year after its release, Beck spoke candidly about its recording: "It's just the worst vocal. I was pretty much making up the song as I was singing it. And I'm not even singing it."[62]

The album's lead-off single, "Where It's At," exemplifies the new direction that *Odelay* was steering Beck on, equally balancing the melody and the mayhem. It builds from a sleepy Hammond organ riff to the hand-clappin', hip-shakin' chorus, " I got two turntables and a microphone." Finding its foundations in a hodge-podgery of sounds, styles, and syncopations, Beck coaxes a sultry sax solo out of David Brown and adds sample of "Needle to the Groove" by the one and only Mantronix.

On the other end of the sonic spectrum, the two-and-a-half-minute amalgam of British new wave and American indie lo-fi, "Minus," was produced and mixed by Beck, Mario Caldato, Jr. (Beastie Boys, Dandy Warhols, Jon Spencer Blues Explosion) and Brian Paulson (Wilco, Son Volt, Golden Smog). Continuing in the vein explored on "Where It's At" and "The New Pollution" with pedal steel work by Gregory Leisz (Grant Lee Buffalo, Matthew Sweet, Brian Wilson), "Sissyneck" captures Beck's uncanny ability to attach appealingly nonsensical lyrics to a mix matchery of styles that makes you boogie oogie oogie, as Ween would say. The song contains elements of "The Moog and Me" by the most awkwardly named performer of all time, Dick Hyman, as well as elements of "A Part of Me" by Paris/Taylor.

With a stoner's lollop, the lulling ditty "Readymade" slips and slides along like a starry-eyed hitchhiker with a sample courtesy of Antonio Carlos Jobim's "Desafinado" performed by Laurindo Almeida and the Bossa Nova All Stars. "['Readymade'] has to do with being a sentient being in a business that requires you to be a machine that's sensitized and human to an extreme, yet is capable of dispensing energy and emotion on demand," Beck explains. "When you're meeting eighty people a day and swimming in a fast-moving river of faces and conversations, then playing for an audience every night, and living on a schedule that tells you where you're gonna be in six months, to the hour, part of you wants to just surrender and go through the motions. I still try to make connections and feel related to where I am, but it's a struggle."[63]

For all their structural simplicity and folksy acoustics, "High Five (Rock the Catskills)" and "Ramshackle" very well could have been on *Mellow Gold*. The first borrows a clip from Rasputin's Stash's "Mr. Cool" to complete its vibe, while the latter conjures memories of *Mellow Gold*'s "Blackhole." "Ramshackle" was the only track kept from the Rothrock and Schnapf sessions (though others would turn up as B-sides).

One of the more interesting tunes laid to tape during the *Odelay* sessions was a soulful, epic jam known as "I Wanna Get With You (and Your Sister Debra)" that had been a tour encore staple since 1996. Eventually, it was decided that its smooth R&B vibe didn't gel with the overall feeling of *Odelay*, but the song would later rear its head during the *Midnite Vultures* sessions.

All that was left to do was package and title the thirteen-song collection. Beck had initially entitled the album *Órale*, which roughly translates into "right on" in Spanish, but an engineer transcribed it incorrectly as *Odelay* on a CD of the final mix. When Beck saw the mistake, he dug it and the name stuck. *Odelay*'s cover art nicks a pic from 1979's *The Golden Anniversary Edition: The Complete Dog Book* and is a sheep dog of Tibetan descent named Komondor. "I was looking at this dog book, and I came to a picture of the most extreme dog," Beck remembered smiling. "He looked like a bundle of flying udon noodles attempting to leap over a hurdle. I couldn't stop laughing for about twenty minutes. Plus the deadline for the cover was a day away."[64] Some of Al's art was included on the insert as an unofficial tribute, as were the works of sociopolitical Philippine painter Manuel Ocampo.

Listening back to the final mixes, Beck and his labels knew they had a special project on their hands—*Odelay* was a groundbreaking album of epic proportions. Not only was the collection a drastic departure from *Mellow Gold*, but its singular sound was unlike anything that had come across the musical marketplace *ever*. As accessible as the hooks, melodies, and choruses were, all parties involved knew that Beck's artistic creed still hung in the balance and that his image and promotion would have to be carefully managed.

CHAPTER 5

Suburban Hymns

"I was sick of all the negativity in grunge music. I wanted to do
something creative and affirming, that had a life force to it."

To prep the release of his all-eyes-are-on-me sophomore album, Beck did
press tours of his two strongest European markets, England and Germany, before dropping *Odelay* in the States on June 18, 1996. Despite
label fears that critics might slam the disc, *Odelay* was greeted with the kind of
praise and adulation that "important" albums deserve. *Rolling Stone* expounded,
"For his unaffected exuberance, fervent eclecticism, precocious ingenuity and
stubborn refusal to take himself too seriously, Beck Hansen is rock 'n' roll's
Man of the Year—even if he looks as if he's only twelve years old."[65] *Newsweek* attempted to describe Beck's new direction: "This is American eclectic
music, a '90s analogue to the genre-smooshing slumgullion of Bob Wills, Elvis
Presley or Bob Dylan. Like Dylan, Beck admires Woody Guthrie and plays solo
acoustic sets. But he's got rap and postpunk rock in his head, and uses the
collaging technologies of hip-hip—both electronic sampling and old-school
turntable-futzing."[66] *Billboard* dared not define, letting their parting words say
it all: "A work that reveals an obsession with offbeat sounds and a singular

talent for weaving them into a musically com-pelling whole."

Even the mail-order empire Columbia House would go on to declare the album one of the Top 25 alternative must-have albums of all time. In his summation of the groundbreaker, Christopher Shores wrote: "Not since the birth of the punk ethic has an artist approached making records in such an innovative way as this Kansan-turned-Angelino; like a curious wanderer coming across objects found on a stroll through forgotten streets, Beck unaffectedly tosses in bits of folk, hip-hop, indie rock, jazz, coun-try, blues, cinematic strings, electronic, easy listening, experimental noise, funk and soul into *Odelay*'s seamless and thoroughly pop-savvy take on rock and roll."[67] "Beck is what Bob Dylan was ages ago," *The New York Times Magazine* editorial director Gerald Marzorati wrote. "He's the singer/songwriter you could do a term paper on. You could write that Beck's approach to music evinces a comprehension of bricolage and the impossibility of aesthetic originality in a postmodern moment of information overload."[68]

The artist Momus was blown away by *Odelay*'s artistic connotations and implications. "Beck put artificiality over authenticity, he brought freaky performance art values to indie. He did successfully what I was trying to do in the late eighties, which is to come in as an outsider with love and hate for pop in equal measure and start making postmodern parodies of the sound of pop-ular music, parodies which reflect your ambivalence by making it sound kind of weird and skewed, horrible and sick. I did this with a morally queasy form of variété-savvy disco, Beck used rapped-up folk. Beck parodied the notion of the authentic, and the Dust Brothers's production highlighted the arbitrariness of his approach to musical style."[69]

Despite five-star reviews and glistening cut-quotes, Beck wasn't lis-tening to critics. The artist had learned all too painfully that critics would shun him one minute and enshrine him the next. "It's something I don't get hung up on, because they change their mind so much."[70] Fans were just as eager to hear Beck's newest creation, and the album debuted at #16 on the *Billboard*

Top 200. By late August it had gone gold and would go on to sell more than two million copies in the U.S. and another several million in foreign territories. "Where It's At" was chosen as the first single and easily ascended *Billboard*'s Modern Rock Tracks to #5. Somewhat of a crossover hit, though to no extent as widely as "Loser," it hit #40 on the Hot 100 Singles Airplay chart—just high enough that Casey Kasem would count it down one week. Overseas, the song charted well in the U.K., Australia, and Japan, becoming an international summer anthem.

For the folks at MTV, Hansen and Hanft hooked up for a fourth time. The video clip, which took three days to shoot in the Cali desert, opens with a sunrise and a mirrored-glasses cop enjoying a cup of java. Then there's Beck working in the road crew, Beck singing onstage at the used-car dealership, Beck in a tuxedo, and finally Beck leading a country-and-western band while line dancers cut the rug. You can spot Eddie from Sukia again (he first appeared in the "Loser" clip as the longhaired, bare-chested rocker)—he's the one holding oranges in front of his eyes in the last sequence. The video contains several intentional references for sharp-eyed fans—the opening shot of the state trooper mimics *Cool Hand Luke* and the faux poetry-slam sequence mockingly imitates William Shatner's spoken-word readings of Elton John tunes.

Considering the sometimes disastrous results of his *Mellow Gold* tour dates, Beck was eager to prove himself as an entertaining performer and competent musician. The songs and arrangements were now incredibly complex, and Beck wanted the stage show to reflect his coming of age. "An audience needs for somebody to get up there and be a complete idiot," Beck asserts. "If a thousand people are gonna go out of their way to buy tickets and be down with you, you gotta represent. You gotta give it back five times!"[71] To begin, he did a pair of Cali dates and a lone gig for the Canucks before he headed off to regale the European summer-festival circuit with his new tunes. Beck talked to Britain's *The Face* about how his foreign audiences seemed to be "getting it," even if they didn't get his train of reference and influence. "Well y'know it doesn't really matter what they think of how and where the shit developed, y'see. The moves are encoded and the message they vibe on is how the ladies

Can I get a hallelujah? PHOTO COURTESY OF SCOTT GRIES/IMAGEDIRECT

are strong and need to be respected by the mens. It's like ESP up there. I see it in their eyes during the gig that they're getting the funky word, y'know?"[72] Still relying on the slap-dash spirits of spontaneity and irreverence, Beck's gigs were transformed into spectacles of rock-god proportion, combining elements of Elvis's stage moves, a preacherman's zeal, ironic rock posturing, and a night out at the Apollo Theatre.

But Beck wasn't your typical rock 'n' roll star. In fact, he wanted nothing more than to mock the conventions of the usual Bic lighter–waving and fireworks-studded encores that fans had come to expect of their MTV icons. Despite the care he put into his live shows, he found touring a draining and daunting task, and *Odelay* brims with references to motion, travel, and road weariness. Beck attaches a certain reluctance and despondence to his forays into the slogging life of a touring musician, as on "Readymade": "An open road where I can breathe/Where the lowest low is callin' to me." It's the feeling of the inevitability of movement that Beck seems to be addressing, perhaps jabbing more than one finger at his record company's ceaseless insistence to tour. He opens "Jack-Ass" with the lines, "I've been drifting along in the same stale old shoes/Loose ends tying a noose in the back of my mind." Beck balances this dislike for travel with his yearning for stability on "Derelict": "I dropped my anchor in the dead of night/I packed my suitcase and threw it away."

As this newfound critic's darling came to terms with his mistrust of the role he had been forced to play, Beck continued to hone his live presence. To best remedy the situation, he came back to the States to spend April incessantly gigging. Slowly but surely, the venues got larger and the sellouts were quicker. After a month off, Beck loaded up the ponies and headed to Japan for a string of sold-out dates. In the midst of preaching to the converted, Geffen culled "Devils Haircut" as the second single and paired Beck up with his first big-name video director, Mark Romanek. The acclaimed director, who had recently won a Grammy for his work on Janet Jackson's "Got Till It's Gone," had carved some memorable images into the pop-culture timeline. One of the definitive video directors who helped style the MTV look, Romanek is responsible for everything from Michael and Janet Jackson's seven-million-dollar

"Scream" clip to Nine Inch Nails's disturbing "Closer" vid and the CK anorexia feel of Fiona Apple's "Criminal." His visual take on "Devils Haircut" pays homage to François Truffaut's classic *The 400 Blows* and John Schlesinger's *Midnight Cowboy,* as a boom-box-totin' Beck struts through the streets of New York City past Grand Central Station, Times Square, Coney Island, and Chinatown. The tune hit a modest #23 on the Modern Rock Tracks chart in early November, while MTV did their part by ceaselessly spinning the clip.

Over in the U.K., Noel Gallagher of Oasis personally asked Beck if he could remix "Devils Haircut." "I felt very honored by Noel's interest," Beck later said. "I would never think that he would have the time to do something like that. I mean, I wouldn't even have time to remix one of my own songs, no matter how much I liked it."[73] In return, Gallagher replied without his usual cutting sarcasm, "Beck's a hero of mine. Hopefully, there will be more collaborations in the future."[74] Is Beck truly a fan of the brothers Gallagher and their mysterious "Wonderwall," though? Talking to Thurston Moore for *The Face,* Beck said, "Whatever, of course I like Oasis. They are the perfect namesake to their vibe, an oasis cannot be dealt with in reality 'cuz it's illusionary. You must beware oasis but you may enjoy the potential of the fantasy and deliverance they offer."[75] In the same interview, he offered up his opinion on the then fabulously popular Spice Girls. "I like their hits, that's all I've heard. I haven't checked out their non-hits. There's nothing wrong with being a Spice Girl. Why does a musician have to be so down and hep to be valid, y'know? It's OK to be a tacky souvenir."[76]

When the December issues hit newsstands, *Odelay* continued to be a resounding winner with the critics. No longer did there seem to be a divide between the believers and the skeptics. Now there were only converts and I-told-you-so's. The album topped *Rolling Stone*'s "10 Best Albums of 1996," *SPIN*'s "20 Best Albums of 1996" list, *The Village Voice* "Pazz & Jop Critics' Poll," and *NME*'s "1996 Critic's Poll." Perhaps even more validating, fellow artists like Bob Dylan, Bono, Damon Albarn of Blur, Cypress Hill, and Snoop Doggy Dogg gave the album props in their year-end best-of lists. These awards were an authentication of Beck's credible and incredible success and proof

The funk soul brother. PHOTO COURTESY OF SCOTT GRIES/IMAGEDIRECT

that he wouldn't be leaving the wasteland of mainstream consciousness any-time soon.

As well as printed pats on the back, Tom Petty paid Beck the ultimate compliment by recording a cover of "Asshole" from *One Foot in the Grave* for the *She's the One* soundtrack. In turn, Beck interviewed the Heartbreakers frontman for the January 1997 cover story of *Musician*. The intriguing dialogue stands as a poignant look inside the ways both of them make art, especially when the two compare notes on their songwriting processes. Petty admitted, "I've never written a song touring, ever. That just stamps it dead for me. I don't feel like playing the guitar. Some people go back to their room or carry portable studios on the road. I couldn't possibly do that. It's always after you come back from the tour and you feel like a civilian." Beck replied, "There's no way. It's all-consuming. You're more on a basic level of existence and survival. It's about trying to get five or six hours of sleep somehow, getting at least one decent meal so you don't just wither away, and dealing with going to the radio station and all this other glamorous stuff [*laughter*]. Trying to find a shirt that you haven't sweated profusely in five nights in a row. Then you go into the stu-dio, it always seems like you're running from scratch again. Everything you thought you had all worked out getting to the next place, you're clueless. It seems like every year you're at a different place. You're not going to be able to make the song you made four years ago."[77]

Another Beck cover came later that year in the form of Johnny Cash's recording of *Stereopathetic Soul Manure's* "Rowboat" for his Rick Rubin–pro-duced *Unchained* album. Backed by the Heartbreakers and a few Fleetwood Mac-ers, the "Man in Black" updated his hipness factor by covering tunes by the likes of Soundgarden, Dean Martin, Tom Petty, and a few country standards for good measure.

The jubilant new year began with Beck's first-ever *Saturday Night Live* appearance on January 11 to perform "Where It's At" and "The New Pollu-tion." In between performances, Beck made his TV acting debut in a skit about medicinal marijuana with host Kevin Spacey and Monty Python–graduate Michael Palin. The following Monday, Beck made a surprise appearance on

The Rosie O'Donnell Show to clue the talk-show hostess into some hip lingo and the signs o' the times. That same day, he stopped by Howard Stern's "Birthday Bash" to serenade the usual host of transvestites, porn stars, and midgets with "Where It's At" and "Novacane."

During this stream of appearances, Beck invaded newsstands everywhere with his debut *SPIN* cover, dubbed "Artist of the Year." One might think that this would be a source of pleasure for an artist coming into his own, but it was somewhat the opposite. Talking several years later to the *NME,* Beck was asked whose ass he would most like to exact some revenge upon. He replied with a tongue-in-cheek *Beverly Hills Cop* reference: "When I did a *SPIN* cover about three or four years ago the photographer airbrushed my face with all kinds of crazy makeup, made me look like some goth clown. So at the time, I very much wanted revenge. I would have done something indirect. A banana up the tailpipe."[78] Indeed, the picture makes Beck look like a cross between David Bowie in *The Man Who Fell to Earth* and a *Quadrophenia* scooter boy who had just done a sheet of blotter acid. However, when Beck finally got the *Rolling Stone* cover he deserved in April of that year, their photo editor decided to go with a far more tasteful and well-executed black-and-white shot that accentuated Beck's boyish visage and sardonic demeanor.

Despite his hectic schedule of gigs, TV shows, and interviews, Beck chose to direct the video clip for his next single himself. His highly stylized endeavor for "The New Pollution" contains a postmodern mishmash of references to the Beatles, the Who, *American Bandstand,* Mötley Crüe, Kraftwerk, *Hullabaloo,* and *Shindig.* The song itself was a reaction to another cultural movement and aesthetic, as he told *People:* "I was sick of all the negativity in grunge music. I wanted to do something creative and affirming, that had a life force to it."[79] Beck expressed this vibrancy both in the song and the look he had begun to adopt over the course of the world tour for *Odelay,* a more refined style involving Mod-like fitted suits, ruffled shirts, cowboy hats, patent leather shoes, and whatever else struck his fancy. His girlfriend Leigh was a clothing designer and had a lot to do with shaping Beck's new look, almost a polar opposite of the look he had cultivated during the *Mellow Gold* years.

Snappy dresser. PHOTO COURTESY OF SCOTT GRIES/IMAGEDIRECT

Peaking at #9 on the *Billboard* Modern Rock Tracks chart in April, "The New Pollution" lingered for twenty weeks on the countdown. The tune would be his biggest hit to date in the U.K., hitting #14 on their pop charts. The label peeps in the U.K. packaged the single as a two-parter containing an Aphex Twin remix entitled "Richard's Hairpiece," a remix of the A-side by Mario C. & Mickey P., and two previously unreleased ditties, the Sonic Youth-esque experimentalist track "Electric Music and the Summer People" and "Lemonade," which was recorded back in March of 1994 with Brian Paulson at the helm. Beck obliged his faithful Brit brat legions by flying over to perform "The New Pollution" on *Top of the Pops* on March 7, 1997, alongside Aerosmith, No Doubt, and the Bee Gees.

For the final U.S. single from the album, Beck decided to return to the capable hands of Steve Hanft for the "Jack-Ass" clip. Filmed primarily in black-and-white, Beck plays a listless coal miner strolling through a dimly lit mine shaft. In one surreal moment, Willie Nelson wheels by in a trolley dressed as a wizard to throw magic stardust at Beck. At the end of the video, our dust-covered hero emerges from the dirty underground, and the film stock changes to color. If any of the scenes look familiar, your sharp eye may have recognized the Batcave where the original *Batman* series was filmed.

Geffen notched up another hit when the song climbed to #15 on *Billboard's* Modern Rock Tracks in September 1997. To commemorate the single and to squeeze some more hard-earned dollars from fans, the label pressed up a CD single full of rarities. The EP included Butch Vig's mix of the A-side, "Burro" (a mariachi-styled take on "Jack-Ass"), "Strange Invitation" (an orchestral take on "Jack-Ass"), and the heretofore unheard piano miniballad "Brother," which was recorded with Tom and Rob back in early 1995. But this wasn't enough for Geffen U.K., and so a few months after the release of "Jack-Ass" in Britain, "Sissyneck" was released as a single backed by a remix of "The New Pollution" by Mickey P. and "Feather in Your Cap." The latter tune originally appeared on the *subUrbia* soundtrack and was recorded during the original *Odelay* sessions with Tom and Rob back in October 1994 at the Shop.

There's nothing like going on the road to promote an album with a seemingly endless string of singles. So Beck dutifully climbed into the tour

Ticket stub:

```
EVENT          SUBJECT TO THE CONDITIONS ON THE BACK HEREOF    EVENT        ADMIT ONE
A11     A11                    BECK                            A11          19.80
P                        W/ THE CARDIGANS                                   BBBBBB
SEC   ADMISSION      THURS 5-22-97 7PM ALL AGE      SEC
          ONE        RED ROCKS AMPHITHEATRE
ROW    PRICE              RAIN OR SHINE             ROW
GENs  19.80              PRODUCED BY NIPP           GEN
          00025  10  CITY TAX INC 002062                      BBBBBB
ADM    4 23  SEC   ROW GEN  ADM  19.80  SEAT   ADM            603063
SEAT                   SEAT       ADMISSION       SEAT    NO REFUND/EXCHANGE
```

bus and hawked his tunes like an ancient herb peddler wearily showing off his mystical array of wares. From February through April he embarked on his most extensive, intensive, and expansive American tour ever, playing theaters, arenas, and large auditoriums for three months straight. Then he hit the European festival circuit again, where he wowed English fans at the Glastonbury Festival by performing in a mariachi outfit. Upon return Stateside he set out on his most unorthodox road trip to date—a choice slot on the H.O.R.D.E. (Horizons of Rock Developing Everywhere) Festival alongside Neil Young, Kula Shaker, Primus, Ween, and Ben Folds Five. Even more diverse than the Lolla lineup, the faux hippie tour failed to match previous years' earnings, and tickets sales were lackluster.

Beck's interactions with bling-bling rap stars were even less successful than his crossover marketing into the H.O.R.D.E. world of Hackey sacks, tie-dyes, and Blues Traveler wannabes. Record company mogul and rap maven Puff Daddy called upon Beck to provide some alterna-rock flavor to his upcoming project *Forever*. Studio time was booked, and Beck found himself in Boyz II Men's personal studio getting ready to freestyle for Puffy over a loop of Elton John's "Bennie and the Jets." "They heard the track, they were grooving to it, their necks were moving, they were on it," Beck begins. "Then I started singing about, like, how expensive my hormones were. The necks froze. Sour looks crossed the faces. And they were gone, they were out." He laughs. "And so was I."[80] "It wasn't even a song, it was a failed experiment.... In a diplomatic way, we were shown the door."[81]

At the end of the summer, Beck made two final calls to the continent across the Atlantic to play a pair of festivals before grounding himself on

Beck plays the MTV Video Music Awards. PHOTO COURTESY OF SCOTT GRIES/IMAGEDIRECT

American soil for the remainder of the year. When the MTV Video Music Award nominees were announced, not only was Beck nominated across the board, he was also set to perform. Two days before the big gig, Beck paid a visit to the Ed Sullivan Theater to perform "Jack-Ass" for the Beck-hungry *Late Show with David Letterman* audience. Afterward, the always-clever performer sat down with Dave and proceeded to take credit for creating the Hanson brothers, claiming they were a product of his intense meditation.

On September 4, Beck rolled up to the red carpet of Radio City Music Hall for the MTV Awards ready to wow the mixed crowd of industry heavy-weights, lucky contest winners, and fellow artists, including Marilyn Manson, U2, Prodigy, and Beck's failed collaborator, Puff Daddy. Beck's hyper-colored and meticulously executed performance of "The New Pollution" was a show-stopper as the singer combed his hair, waved a fan, cracked a whip, and thrust his hips. Beck ended up taking the stage regularly that night as he walked away with the moon men awards for Best Male Video and Best Editing for "Devils Haircut," and the Best Direction in a Video, Best Choreography, and Best Art Direction in a Video awards for "The New Pollution."

Two days later, Beck officially completed the *Odelay* world trek with one last stop at the *Sessions at West 54th* studio. In full preacher mode, the tour-tuned maestro blazed through a rousing setlist that went from the frantic falsettos of "I Wanna Get With You (and Your Sister Debra)" to the hand-clapping crescendos of "Where It's At." This show demonstrated just how far Beck had come from reclusive solo artist to talented bandleader and peerless performer.

To commemorate his globe-spanning tramp, Beck released a glossy souvenir book entitled *Travels* for fans. The slender paperback was a collection of photos from the course of the tour, shot mostly by Charlie Gross and Michael Halsband, but with several contributions from his girlfriend Leigh and Autumn deWilde. Beck penned a characteristically quirky intro to the tome:

> We vibrate. We reverberate. We are Beck. We are not a club, committee, or a subsidiary. We are a miasmic enterprise; a time zone synchronized with dead oceans. Upon entering our area, you are no longer a visitor, nor a spectator. You are a participant in a crude experiment. Once fulfilled, this experiment cancels itself out, the only vestige life—these photographs. Let them warm you like the embers from a once noxious conflagration.

Though the tour was officially finished, Beck and his boys made a few sporadic appearances, including Farm Aid on October 4. After running through country-fried versions of "Leave Me on the Moon," "Rowboat," "Ramshackle," and "Jack-Ass," Beck joined Willie Nelson on a cover of Jimmie Rodgers's

"Peach Pickin' Time in Georgia," a tune they would later cover together on *The Tonight Show.*

The old-school establishment had obviously been tuned into the Beck sensation. On December 16, a lone Beck opened one of Bob Dylan's five nights at the El Rey Theatre in L.A. His half-hour acoustic set served as a preview of his forthcoming acoustic album, *Mutations,* plying new creations like "Cold Brains" and "Dead Melodies," alongside older tunes like "Waitin' for a Train," "Girl Dreams," "Leave Me on the Moon," "I Get Lonesome," "One Foot in the Grave," and "Lampshade."

Odelay had such an extended cycle of success that Beck once again raked in the kudos during the year-end wrap-ups. The suave operator swept the *Rolling Stone* Reader's Poll, taking "Best Album" for *Odelay,* "Best Alternative Artist," #2 "Favorite Artist" (behind Smashing Pumpkins), #3 "Best Video" for "Where It's At," and #5 in the "Five Best Singles" category, also for "Where It's At."

For the second time in his career, Beck received several nods from the Grammy folks. This time Beck walked home with something to proudly—if not sarcastically—display above his fireplace when he nailed the Best Alternative Music Performance Grammy for *Odelay* and the Best Male Rock Vocal Performance for "Where It's At." However, he lost the golden gramophone for Album of the Year to Celine Dion's *Falling Into You.*

Normally this massive accomplishment would have signaled the end of the gigantic whirlwind of promotion and touring for *Odelay,* which had consumed over a year and a half of Beck's life. However, the ever-prolific artist wasn't content to rest on the laurels of *Odelay,* so he penned a track entitled "Deadweight" for the soundtrack to the movie *A Life Less Ordinary.* Brought to you by the same crazed geniuses responsible for *Trainspotting,* the genre-spanning soundtrack features musical contributions from Ash, Luscious Jackson, Underworld, Folk Implosion, and even Elvis. "Deadweight" was chosen as the first single from the collection, and Beck decided to work with director Michel Gondry for the clip. Gondry's résumé included a variety of electronica pioneers, from Daft Punk and Bjork to the Chemical Brothers's pairing with Noel Gallagher, "Let Forever Be," which garnered him an MTV Breakthrough Video award. The imaginative concept clip for "Deadweight" finds a discombobulated Beck floating in and out of scenes from *A Life Less Ordinary,* attempting to rationalize reality with cinematic wizardry. The tune hit #16 on *Billboard's* Modern Rock Tracks in January and remained an alt-rock radio staple all winter. Overseas, the label packaged the A-side with "Erase the Sun" and "SA-5," two minimalist compositions which could easily have been on *Stereopathetic Soul Manure.*

Meanwhile, Beck was convinced by his label to revive his road fever and begin another stretch of touring in Australia and New Zealand. Then, in May and June, he did a few select European dates and California headlining gigs before opening up for the Dave Matthews Band on a string of stadium shows. "I remember getting the sense from the audience that they really didn't believe we were a real band. There were a lot of people pointing at us and then looking inquisitively at one another. I don't think it really registered that we were actually playing music."[82] Despite Dave Matthews's personal love of Beck, it was generally received as an awkward and somewhat unsuccessful pairing.

After canceling an appearance at the Tibetan Freedom Concert in Washington, D.C., when lightning struck and injured eleven fans, Beck rarely took the stage for the remainder of the year. However, in October, he paused from his other commitments to play Silicon Planet's AIDS benefit. Though he loathes corporate events, Beck publicly admitted he had been coaxed to perform at various convention-styled settings in order to relieve the enormous debt brought on by constant touring. "I don't really like to do those kinds of things. I've never done anything for Miller [Beer] or any of those corporations. We did a couple of shows for some computer firms around the time of *Odelay,* but only because I was in debt from touring. I tend to lose money on the road. Most bands don't make money unless you're at the level of Dave Matthews or Smashing Pumpkins. So I did some of the shows, but they're not really my thing. At the same time, I'm supporting a lot of people here. These guys are like my family, and I've got to take care of them. But when I'm asked to do stuff like the *Austin Powers* soundtrack, things that just seem gross, I stay away. I

First of all, I'd like to thank God ... PHOTO COURTESY OF FRANK MICELOTTA/IMAGEDIRECT

get asked to put my music in a Toyota commercial for ungodly sums of money, and as a rule, I stay away from most of it."[83] Interestingly, during the recording of *Midnite Vultures,* Beck used his appearance at HSX/Excite's post-Oscar party to road test a couple of new tunes.

Over the course of his touring breaks that spring and summer, Beck and his brother, Channing, got involved in promoting his grandfather's artistic legacy. Curator and collector Wayne Baerwaldt posthumously assembled a traveling collection and subsequent book on the Hansen family's artistic process entitled *Playing With Matches.* Baerwaldt told *L.A. Weekly,* "We wanted to convey Al's vitality as a long-term, twenty-four-hour-a-day performer who inspired Beck's showmanship and free-form style."[84] The book and tour were also a chance to elevate Al Hansen to the status his family always felt he deserved. "He was on the cusp of breaking through in America before he died, and he died a little too soon," Beck mused. This was their chance to "finish the work he was doing."[85]

When Beck's and his grandfather's art were physically laid side-by-side, there were a striking number of similarities. Wayne Baerwaldt compares the two artists in *Beck & Al Hansen: Playing With Matches:*

> What Beck and Al share is an eclectic rummaging for common materials and a propensity for sampling and juxtaposing choice bits with a sensitivity to the "magic" in art-making. The most recognizable, shared feature in this process is an economy of means. Their materials are predominantly refuse, the images, objects and sounds that most people throw away or ignore, considered too rudimentary, unsophisticated and often too insignificant for recycling. In unexpected combinations of subject matter and materials, their works tread a fine line between visual art objects and art as conceptual ideas.[86]

The first exhibition of *Playing With Matches* took place at the Santa Monica Museum of Art. Opening on May 7, Beck performed a Happening in his grandfather's memory entitled *New Age Evisceration I*. Beck was backed by a band called the Dream Weavers (a reference to Gary Wright's hit tune that *Wayne's World* references) and decked to the nines in hippie garb. The show/performance art piece included a dolphin wielding a giant strap-on penis and Beck power-sawing his keyboard in half as the finale. At the opening at the Schoss Moyland Museum in Bedburg-Hau, Germany, Channing delighted the crowd with several performances, including a recreation of *Yoko Ono Piano Drop*. Later, at the Vancouver unveiling, Channing wrapped his head in masking tape—a stunt his grandfather created called *Elegy for the Fluxus Dead*. "[It's] a piece that I inherited from my grandfather after his death," Channing stated. "I read a list of Fluxist artists who have died. And then I wrap my head up in tape simultaneously with the projection of my grandfather wrapping his head up in tape. We do it—it's our collaborative piece."[87]

It was a relief for Beck to be able to exercise another side to his artistic ability. "I finally got off tour [after] two years, and I started doing some [art] again. I was having a hard time settling back down into my life, and working

on these was good for my sanity. I ended up making a bunch of new pieces."[88] But he was reluctant to show these latest pieces—he thought they looked too new and not mature enough. In fact, Beck wasn't sure about the next time he would hold a gallery showing of his artwork. "Not for a while. Maybe in twenty years. Most of my creative energy [in the near future] will go into the albums and the live show and the visual stuff for that. My next tour will have more sets and more of an installation effect."[89]

All told, the extensive promotion for *Odelay* had taken up over two years of Beck's life. The prolonged and worldwide success of *Odelay* catapulted Beck even higher into the stratosphere of pop culture, making him a veritable icon. Paparazzi recognized him, fellow artists attempted to mimic his stylings, magazines swooned for the honor of putting him on their covers, and his striking videos were always playing on MTV. He had reached that next plateau where credibility and success went hand-in-hand. And ultimately, he had done it on his own terms.

CHAPTER 6

Ballad of a Thin Man

"People write that I dig through the pickle barrel of the past. But
I think of the music of the last hundred years as contemporary.
It's all part of a fluid continuous line."

Beck needed to recharge his creative cells before recording a proper follow-up to *Odelay*, so as a stop-gap he recorded an album of acoustic works, mostly older songs that had been kicking around even prior to the making of *Odelay*. "I was on the road for about two and a half years, so I didn't really have that many songs. These were songs that have been marinating for the last four years, sort of sitting in the scrapbook."[90]

Conceptually, he wanted to move away from the in-your-face sampling and grooving of *Odelay* and show off his more passive and mellow side. "I'd always wanted to make a record that was just a mood piece. When I get home or I'm at a hotel after a gig, I don't really want to rock out. I don't really want to put on this progressive, electronic Sturm und Drang. The records that I tend to listen to are records that don't hit you over the head. They're like old friends you can just hang out with them. Like early Neil Young or Joni Mitchell's *Blue*. Those kinds of records are pacifying."[91] "I don't really think of it as a step back, it's just a sort of step aside. Everyone and their mother is using a drum loop and samples and integrating dance culture into pop music and I just, you know, I've become wary of becoming a formula."[92]

So, from March 19 to April 3, 1998, during a touring break, he locked himself in Ocean Way Studios to coproduce what would become *Mutations,* along with acclaimed producer Nigel Godrich (Radiohead, Travis) and Beck's touring band. While their schedule was tight, banging out one track a day, the vibe was still loose: "The only thing I had was that the songs were written. On *Mellow Gold* and *Odelay,* most of the songs hadn't been written, I'd go into the studio, just kind of build these songs piece by piece and at the end, the song would be written. So I did everything backward this time, but nobody knew the songs. It was basically myself and several of the musicians set up in a room with mics and there's a couple songs where we did the vocal live."[93]

For the most part, the tracks were recorded live with Beck and whatever musicians were needed, with vocal overdubs added later. To get a feel for the final arrangements, Beck would sometimes scat-sing over the tracks. For the first time, Beck really concentrated on his vocals as an instrument: "The singing has always been an afterthought in other records. It's always the least worked on. I think Nigel is somebody who really encouraged the emotional aspect of the performance to come out. He made it OK for me to be expressive."[94] It was a conscientious choice for Beck to record the album live. "It was just a gut instinct.... I'm not a purist with traditional studio techniques and analog and all that. I recognize the benefits of digital. But there's something about a commitment to laying something on a tape that can't be altered later. It's a moment, and you have to express everything you want in that moment."[95]

There was a strict curriculum for the sessions: arrive early at the studio, practice for twenty minutes, arrange the mics, and then record. Godrich would spend half an hour remixing at the end of the day and then it would be on to the next track. As the last day of recording ticked away its final moments, Nigel was still putting the finishing touches on the last vocal track. As his car service pulled up to take him to his plane, the making of *Mutations* ended.

Looking over the album, Beck referred to *Mutations* in an interview with *The Buffalo News* as "spontaneous and unmediated" with "less pastiche" and as "stripped down and kind of personal."[96] Talking about his inspirations and influences for the album, Beck said, "People write that I dig through the pickle barrel of the past. But I think of the music of the last hundred years as contemporary. It's all part of a fluid continuous line. People have a general sense of superiority to the past, but I don't think we're any smarter or more enlightened. We were still the same people eighty years ago as we were twenty years ago. I also think that when you come to the end of something you really have to go back to the beginning."[97]

At the end of the brief recording period, there were eleven songs listed on the sleeve and one hidden bonus track, "Diamond Bollocks." *Mutations* opens with "Cold Brains," a plaintive ditty that swirls with its own private majesty. Beck's dad stepped into the studio to arrange and conduct strings for the next song, "Nobody's Fault But My Own," as well as "We Live Again," which cops the opening riff from Louis Armstrong's "What a Wonderful World."

The rambling melody of "Lazy Flies" fits its discursive lyrics, as Beck flits between images of a gloved magistrate to puritans, robots, gigolos, and matrons. The strange sounds that greet the listener on "Canceled Check" are all sorts of shit flying around the studio—from coffee cups to salt 'n' pepper shakers. "The song was sort of dying out, and we didn't really know how to end it—so we just all went into the room and took all the [percussion] stuff, shakers and coffee cups, and things were just flying. There was this melee of studio gear—and people got hurt actually."[98] "Canceled Check" is one of the oldest songs on the record and had been receiving live airings since the days of the first *Mellow Gold* tour. It's likely that it would have been recorded for the intended acoustic follow-up to his debut if Beck had gone down that route. The song's inspiration came to him while he was watching a Tony Robbins-esque infomercial preacher who characterized the past as a "canceled check."

The hooky bossa nova beat of "Tropicalia" was inspired by Beck's outspoken love for the likes of Jorge Ben, Caetano Veloso, Gal Costa, and Os

Mutantes (who got a backhanded reference in the album title). These artists were all pioneers of the tropicalia movement that began in Brazil in the late sixties. Despite the upbeat music, Beck delivers a downcast set of lyrics: "You're out of luck/You're singing funeral songs." "It's a good summertime song for the winter," Beck said. "And it kind of reminds me of airplanes."[99]

Although not mentioned specifically, Depression-era California comes to mind from the imagery of "Dead Melodies," as Beck gently plucks out a small symphony of a song. The tune ends with the source of its namesake: "Night birds will cackle/Rotting like apples on trees/Sending their dead melodies to me." For the most part, the lyrics on *Mutations* lean toward the depressed and downhearted, as he demonstrates on "Bottle of Blues": "Ain't it hard, ain't it hard/To want somebody who doesn't want you." He joked to Neil Strauss, "We just wanted to make the gentlemen cry the realistic tears."[100]

Not to be confused with the traditional song "Ave Maria," "O Maria" is a piano-spice jazz song played with Western saloon flair. The next track, "Sing It Again," was originally written for Johnny Cash, but Beck ended up keeping it for himself after falling in love with the tune. Closing out the listed selections is "Static," which opens with the self-loathing couplet, "It's so easy to laugh at yourself/When all those jokes have already been written." The song casually builds to a lazy crescendo of Beck intoning "Begone ... begone ..." before swirling to an understated finished. The unlisted bonus track, "Diamond Bollocks," is the most *Odelay*-esque song on the collection and was originally intended to be the second track. However, Beck decided that the electronica-squiggled, fuzzed-up rocker that stomps and romps like a Sonic Youth-meets-Pavement one-off was too off-kilter with the overall vibe of the collection and moved it to the end.

The album's interior artwork was courtesy of Tim Hawkinson, an L.A.-based artist whose bent for transforming found objects into strange devices and inventions bears an ideological likeness to Al Hansen. One featured sculpture on the album sleeve is a giant fingertip cut and stuffed with red pens, while another is a suspended male form made completely out of transparent plastic and inflated. The third is a uterine landscape with two giant wombs connected with plastic tubes and a dangling figure of a man in between them.

On the flipside of these odd apparitions, Beck fans may have been surprised to find a careful mapping of the collection's lyrics. *Mutations* marked the first time Beck had allowed his lyrics to be reprinted on an album sleeve. Now instead of watching the equalizer bounce with an ear cocked toward the speaker, trying to figure out what the wordsmith was saying, listeners were left with the task of dissecting the real meaning behind the lyrics. "I have a twofold relationship [with lyrics]," Beck admitted. "On one hand they're incredibly important. And on the other hand they shouldn't be important at all. It's like drawing a picture that has some balance to it. You don't want to give it too much detail or you'll just get caught up in the details. At the same time, you don't want it to be just a blur."[101]

Though the album was originally slated to be a solely independent release via Bong Load, so as to indicate to fans that it wasn't the "official" follow-up to *Odelay,* Geffen ended up picking up the project and running with it, much to the artist's displeasure and concern. Nonetheless, *Mutations* hit shelves November 3, 1998 bearing the Geffen logo. It debuted at #13 on the *Billboard* Top 200, selling just over seventy-five thousand copies its first week out.

Despite all the reports from the label and artist indicating the sound of *Mutations* was drastically different than that of *Odelay,* fans and the critics couldn't wait to get their hands on the new platter. Beck acknowledged that his various sonic masks might be disorienting for his fans. "Sometimes I have to go solo from myself. I'm sure it confuses some people. A few of them probably enjoy the confusion. I'm sure some people love one half and hate the other."[102] No matter what the expectations were, the reviews were glorious. Ethan Smith of *New York* magazine gushed that it was some of Beck's "subtlest work" and praised its "lush simplicity,"[103] while *Time* wrote "[*Mutations*] is a ruminative album that's more about quiet revelation than sonic revolution."[104] *Raygun* raved, "He's a bluesman, a soulman, a B-boy and a consummate showman, a trailblazer completely removed from petty West Coast/East

Coast or new/old school rivalries. He's 'the enchanting Wizard of Rhythm.' Everybody listens to him—don't front that you don't—but Beck hasn't let his artistic success go to his head."[105] On the other side of the pond in an 8-out-of-10 review, the *NME* wrote, "[*Mutations* finds Beck] replacing the turntable with the acid-rock light wheel, the concrete streets with the long and winding road.... Beck remains the Midas of Cool, but, most importantly, it's his heart that's made of gold."[106] *Billboard* weighed in with a brief review, citing it as "a masterful plot twist by one of the most adventurous artists in recent memory."[107]

Though the album wasn't very heavily promoted by the artist or the label, it quickly gained gold status on December 7. One proper radio single was begrudgingly released, "Tropicalia," which peaked at #21 on the Modern Rock Tracks *Billboard* chart in November, but no video was ever created for it. However, Beck was getting a lot of exposure in another video he inadvertently appears in—the New Radicals clip for their hooky pop single, "You Get What You Give." In the song, lead singer Gregg Alexander namechecks/disses Beck alongside a few other MTV staples including Marilyn Manson and Hanson: "With a brash swagger, Alexander declares/You're all fakes, run to your mansions/Come around, we'll kick your ass in." Interestingly, Alexander never had a chance to make good on the threat as he soon thereafter disbanded the group, after feeling he had been prematurely labeled a one-hit wonder by the press.

For the Australian version of "Tropicalia," Beck added his cover of Skip Spence's "Halo of Gold," as well as the previously unreleased instrumental "Black Balloon" (not to be confused with the sappy Goo Goo Dolls song of the same name). The cover art was part of a mixed-media piece Beck had constructed entitled *Emergency Flag* that displayed multicolored fingers playing a piano.

In one of the few live appearances surrounding *Mutations,* Beck stopped by to visit his old friends at KCRW on the *Morning Becomes Eclectic* show on November 24 for his fifth time. Joined by his touring band—guitarist Smokey Hormel, bassist Justin Meldal-Johnsen, drummer Joey Waronker, key-

boardist Roger Joseph Manning Jr., alto saxophonist David Brown, and baritone saxophonist/trombonist David Ralicke, the septet performed seven tunes
from the recently released album and added a last-minute version of "I Wanna
Get With You (and Your Sister Debra)."

Despite the label's constant requests for him to promote *Mutations,*
not much could separate Beck from busily working on the "true" follow-up to
Odelay. However, he did step out on January 9 to swing by the *Saturday Night
Live* studios to perform "Tropicalia" and "Nobody's Fault But My Own." The
next night he played a low-key show at Town Hall in New York City, where Bob
Dylan had trawled his wares in the sixties. Though he had only announced the
gig three days prior, tickets sold out in ten minutes flat. It was to be one of
Beck's career-defining live shows. In full-band mode Beck delivered all eleven
listed tracks on *Mutations* as well as some other choice tunes, including a
cover of Mississippi John Hurt's version of "Stagger Lee" and Skip James's
"He's a Mighty Good Leader" before closing with "I Wanna Get With You (and
Your Sister Debra)," and leaving the stage.

SonicNet.com noted: "The audience seemed to have brought the right
map, responding with quiet, reserved attention almost unheard of at modern
rock shows. The show didn't have quite the pedagogical ambience of a classic
Pete Seeger folk performance, but it wasn't that far off either."[108] Reynard
Labaguis finished his review of the show by praising "the utter completeness
of the Beck Package: chops, style, freshness, hits, lyrics, melodies, groove, soul
and meaning, all shot through with a very personal vision that still manages to
fit nicely on the family tree of American music. The chorus of *Mutations*'s 'We
Live Again' ends with 'Oh I grow weary of the end.' Well, if Mr. Hansen continues on the trip he's chosen to take, the end seems very far away, indeed."[109]

Later that year, Beck played two May shows at L.A.'s Wiltern Theater
and was the surprise opener for Beth Orton at the El Rey Theater in July. Billed
as "Silverlake Menza" and borrowing Beth's own guitar and harmonica, Beck
reveled the surprised crowd with "Tropicalia," "Nobody's Fault But My Own,"
"Cold Brains," and "Lazy Flies." The Tuesday beforehand, he jumped up onstage
to play a tune with Brazilian musical *sensação* (or "sensation" to his unschooled

Shake your money-maker. PHOTO COURTESY OF SCOTT GRIES/IMAGEDIRECT

American audience) Caetano Veloso, who paid tribute to Beck later in his set by playing an instrumental version of "Tropicalia."

As well as a smattering of live gigs, several other public appearances were in the cards for the reticent artist. The night before the Grammys, Beck presented Neil Young and his wife Pegi with Rock the Vote's Patrick Lippert Award, given to groups and individuals for "embodying the spirit of community activism." The Youngs were being honored for their work in founding Farm Aid and the annual Bridge School benefit, both of which Beck had participated in. The next night, the Recording Academy coaxed Beck into copresenting the Record of the Year award, along with Sarah McLachlan and Puff Daddy, to Celine Dion for her titanic sopfest, "My Heart Will Go On."

Despite their creator's frequent reluctance to show his face outside the studio, there was a bevy of Beck-related goodies to tide over fervent fans. Around the time of *Mutations,* the lavish and comprehensive Beck.com debuted as the official online destination for all things Beck. The site began as the lovechild of fan Evan Torrence (aka Truck) while he was still attending high school in Santa Barbara, California. After catching "Loser" on MTV's *120 Minutes,* he decided to craft an online homage to his new favorite artist. Eventually, his fandom was written up in *Entertainment Weekly* and Beck's tour manager gave the artist himself a peek at it. Impressed with what he saw, Beck flew him to a show as a thank-you. "My initial reaction [when I saw the website] was puzzlement, amazement, laughter," says Beck. "I'd never seen so much information on myself. I learned more about myself than I knew. I did see some other sites at that time—some of them were nice, but they weren't as substantial as his."[110] After several meetings, the tech-savvy music lover was given the go-ahead and became the official webmaster.

There were a couple of audio outputs from the Beck camp during this timeframe as well. The first was Beck's cover of "Halo of Gold" on *More Oar: A Tribute to the Skip Spence Album,* a homage to the crazed genius Alexander "Skip" Spence. Spence cofounded and drummed for Jefferson Airplane before switching to guitar and going on to form the briefly lit flame that was San Francisco's Moby Grape. In 1968, he was diagnosed as a paranoid schizophrenic after attempting to do grievous bodily harm to Moby Grape drummer Don Stevenson, convinced that Stevenson was possessed by Satan. Spence spent six months in a psychiatric ward, writing the entirety of what would be his solo album, *Oar*. Upon release, he hopped on a motorcycle to Nashville, where he recorded the whole album himself in less than a week. The tribute version of the album features contributions from Robert Plant, Mark Lanegan of Screaming Trees, Greg Dulli of the Afghan Whigs, and Tom Waits.

The second significant output was Beck's contribution to *Return of the Grievous Angel: A Tribute to Gram Parsons,* alongside Sheryl Crow, David Crosby, and Victoria Williams. Briefly a member of the Byrds and one of the cofounders of the Flying Burrito Brothers, Parsons went on to be a respected solo artist, creating what he himself dubbed "Cosmic American Music." His library of work has served as a cornerstone influence to the likes of the Jayhawks, Wilco, and Uncle Tupelo. Beck duets with Emmylou Harris on "Sin City," a song Parsons penned with Chris Hillman for the Flying Burrito Brothers's 1970 album, *The Gilded Palace of Sin*.

April found Beck headed to Japan for a two-week tour to strum his *Mutations* tunes. It was the biggest push the album would receive anywhere in the world and stood as a testimony to the Japanese's utter adoration of all things Beck. A three-song EP for "Nobody's Fault But My Own," released to coincide with the sold-out jaunt, featured two bonus rarities, "Diamond in the Sleaze" and "One of These Days." The two extra tunes pin Beck's heart prominently on his sleeve. In "Diamond in the Sleaze" he asks, "Do you want to see me suffering?/How could you let a good thing go?" while on the Waits-ian mini-epic "One of These Days" he promises, "One of these days/I'm gonna love you all my life."

As his successes grew greater over the past several years, Beck became increasingly frustrated with the labels' demands on his time and artistry. His relationship with the labels had eroded to the point of serious instability and frustration on both sides. However, not many spectators would have predicted the following scenario that went down. Immediately after his return from Japan and a one-off Hawaiian show, Beck was slapped with a lawsuit from Geffen and Bong Load for breach of contract. This came as an immediate legal response to the fact the artist had informed them on April 23 that he would no longer be required to fulfill the obligations of his contract. Beck cited section 2855 of the California Labor Code, which restricts the length of personal service contracts to seven years, a tactic previously employed by Metallica, Don Henley, and Toni Braxton. Bong Load and Geffen were unhappy with this turn of events and asked the court to enforce the existing contracts and determine damage against Beck, whom they claimed still owed them four albums.

In response on May 10, Beck countersued the labels for nonpayment of royalties and copyright infringement. Beck's attorney, Jill Berliner, claimed *Mutations* was solely owned by Beck, released by Geffen without his consent, and that he hadn't seen either an advance or royalties for the release, despite the fact it had sold more than one million copies worldwide. The suit stated that "Beck achieved stature as a 'signature' artist for Geffen, before Geffen was crushed by the newly formed monolith known as 'Unigram.'... Upon the creation of Unigram, and in the name of 'corporate downsizing,' Unigram forced to the streets the vast majority of the most talented and beloved executives and staff at Geffen. These displaced individuals were critically important to Geffen's relationship with Beck. They have been replaced by persons unknown to Beck, who apparently have to decided to place improper exploitation of Beck's work above contractual and copyright obligations."[111]

The main crux of the issue was that *Mutations* was recorded on Beck's own dime. He then played the album as a courtesy for several unnamed Geffen executives. The suit maintained that "Geffen decided it must copy *Mutations* for release and distribution for the financially critical Christmas season, although Geffen knew it had no right to do so.... Geffen executives felt added pressure from the forthcoming Unigram merger to book sales of the *Mutations* record album despite its lack of ownership of the sound recording copyright or any other rights in the *Mutations* album."[112] Despite an alleged written complaint from Beck's reps, *Mutations* was released as a fourth-quarter flagship album without any documented permission from the artist himself.

It would take almost six months, but Beck finally came to an out-of-

The Ozz-man cometh. PHOTO COURTESY OF SCOTT GRIES/IMAGEDIRECT

court agreement with his label concerning his past woes and future status. The terms were not publicly disclosed. Looking back at the lawsuit later that year, Beck said, "There are all kinds of weird legal things in the contract, but it wasn't a battle. It was more like paperwork and formalities that needed to get sorted out."[113] He later voiced his opinion on the Polygram-Universal merger by admitting, "It's strange to work with different people now, but I've always operated independently from the record company. They're not involved with the creative process of making my albums. I'd prefer to have more time to be creative and evolve. The stakes are too high for artists, and it's not human to have success after success after success."[114]

It had been a crazy year for Beck, full of sporadic ups and downs. But despite all that had gone wrong, the artist was keeping his mind and soul focused on the making of his next album. The artist considered his forthcoming set the "proper" follow-up to *Odelay,* and he was weighed down with great expectations from fans, critics, the label, and, most importantly, himself.

CHAPTER **7**

Burning of the Midnight Lamp

> "I feel that I just want to come out with something kind of stu-
> pid.... It's not really a time to be precious. It's a time to celebrate
> and embrace the broadest human energy and just ride it."

It's not an easy thing to follow up something as artistically and financially successful as *Odelay,* but Beck was determined not to cop out. To push the envelope completely, the pioneering sonic voyager decided to write and produce the whole album by his lonesome. "I could have very easily come out with another *Odelay* and been finished in a couple of months," Beck acknowledged. "But that would have been obvious and cheap. Besides, I had a very specific thing in my head, and I wasn't willing to stop until it was done. If you hear one single part of the new record, there are probably forty different ideas we tried before choosing that one. At times it felt like we were going to hell and back on each song, but I knew what I wanted. I don't know if that drive is a blessing or a curse...."[115] Beck wasn't concerned about limiting his artistic scope: "Where do you define boundaries about what you should and

76

shouldn't do? Most of me tends to not want to care about doing the wrong thing."[116]

Beck touched on his need to constantly reinvent himself in order for the public to stay interested in his work. "I do feel like I have to prove myself again and again, and sense that the ground beneath me is constantly shifting. People no longer relate to music the way they used to, and there are other options now. The economy is the new entertainment, and music isn't even part of the equation in many people's lives. I read somewhere that the rollerblade industry is bigger than the music business, so I'm a few notches below skating as a cultural force."[117]

What would become a complicated and lavish studio project began humbly with Beck recording demos in his living room on a computer. "I started using computers because they were cheap," he admitted. "I could record a 16-track song in my living room on a hard drive. I didn't even have to pay for a tape machine. I'd be the first person to say analog tape sounds a hundred thousand times better than anything digital, but the computer enables me to do all kinds of music I couldn't afford otherwise. This album would have cost millions to make in a conventional studio."[118]

Moving from the living room to the studio was no big step—Beck's studio was built into his new $1.3 million Pasadena pad where he and his girl Leigh had moved from Los Feliz in the spring of 1998 (though they ended up moving back after the album was finally completed). Dubbed Soft Studios, it would be his home at home for the next twelve months. Comparing this process with the making of *Odelay*, Dust Brother Mike Simpson said, "Every day we were starting from scratch [during the recording of *Odelay*]. I think, on *Midnite Vultures*, Beck had written songs before he got to the studio. And this time he had a better grasp of the technology."[119]

Beck's mastery of the technology was a large part of his newfound artistic process, as was his collaborators' ability to keep up with him. After recording wrapped, coproducers Tony Hoffer and Mickey Petralia (Luscious Jackson, Dandy Warhols) talked to *Guitar Player* about the process: "Normally, we had about two and a half minutes to set up," Petralia commented. "Stuff happens really quickly. We shove a mic in front of a speaker, run back to the board, and start dialing things." Hoffer added, "Beck is very creative and very fast. His mind is going ten thousand miles per second. You have to be ahead of him—and that's usually not possible. When you're setting mics up, he's already practicing some riff, and if you aren't recording right then, you risk losing *the* riff. He's also really into the first take or two—the ones where he and the musicians are just learning the parts, and there are all these honest mistakes. Those takes have a certain funkiness that you just can't duplicate, and that's why it's so important to get the sounds dialed in quickly and have everything rolling and ready to go."[120]

After the completion of *Mutations* in July of 1998, Beck had begun to assemble a core group of contributors for his next opus, including bass player Justin Meldal-Johnsen (Medicine, Tori Amos, Air), keyboardist Roger Joseph Manning Jr. (Moog Cookbook, Air), and coproducers/engineers Mickey Petralia and Tony Hoffer. Additional players were called in as necessary—Joey Waronker (R.E.M., Smashing Pumpkins, Elliot Smith) drummed, Smokey Hormel (Lotus Eaters, Bruce Willis, Sam Phillips) laid down the guitar lines, David Brown (the Creatures, Ben Lee) played tenor sax, David Ralicke (Brazzaville, Natalie Merchant) manned the trombone, and Jon Birdsong (Brass Monkey, Brokeback) filled out the horn section on trumpet. All of the musicians involved had either toured or recorded with Beck before, which kept the studio atmosphere friendly and relaxed.

With the players assembled, the songs loosely constructed, and the critics waiting for *Odelay* Version 2.0 to *oooh* and *aaah* over, Hansen took a complete left turn. He wanted to make a bangin' party album. "You know, I'm just wary of this whole millennial overload," Beck said at one point during the recording. "I feel with the millennium, people are coming out with their statement and their summation and trying to extract something meaningful and poignant with this whole culmination of the century and the millennium and all that. And I feel that I just want to come out with something kind of stupid.... It's not really a time to be precious. It's a time to celebrate and embrace the broadest human energy and just ride it."[121]

A flippant record was actually hard for Beck to make. "I find it more of a challenge to make music that's fun. It's very easy for me to make music that's reflective and melancholy. It's hard to make music that's fun but isn't cheap, that isn't just banal and thoughtless."[122] To solidify his commitment to jocularity, during the creation of the album Beck told reporters that he was going to title it *I Can Smell the VD in the Club Tonight,* a lyric he whispers in the middle of "Milk & Honey." After sorting through the forty-plus recorded tunes, Beck had before him his most lighthearted and groovy album to date. Despite the overflow of creativity and funkiness, Beck told MTV it was really only half the record that he wanted to put out and that he'd like to follow it up within a year.

Midnite Vultures opens with a Stax Records horn romp, some killer steel guitar, and a banjo solo that would put Bela Fleck to shame. Perhaps the freakiest single in the Beck discography, "Sexx Laws" has an infectiously twisted pop hook and unorthodox arrangement that *SPIN* gleefully dubbed "an exuberant update to the block-rocking psychedelica of *Odelay.*"[123] The lyrical inspiration came to him suddenly one night on the *Odelay* tour. During an orgiastic jam of the encore "I Wanna Get With You (and Your Sister Debra)," Beck dropped to his knees like it was amateur night at the Apollo and began to scream, "I want to defy the logic of all sex laws!" This moment of spontaneous wordplay stuck with him and became the catchphrase of *Midnite Vultures*'s lead-off single.

The second track, "Nicotine & Gravy," is actually the amalgam of five song ideas that Beck eventually collapsed into one over-the-top number. With Dad handling the string arrangements and a full complement of musicians lending their hands to the mayhem, the song begins in a slow funk and builds to an overwhelming mishmash of dislocated styles with Beck lending the falsetto plea "I don't want to die tonight."

"Mixed Bizness" is another junction of style and sound. *NME* wrote a loving review of the song: "Argue all you want about the po-mo ironic layers of young Mr. Hansen's art-driven dog-and-pony show, but this funkatronic slow-jam from *Midnite Vultures* packs a hefty whack of Jacuzzi-shagging, limo-riding, pimp-rolling superfly kool.... Barmier than Bootsy Collins, ruder than Rick James, plusher than a shag-pile carpet in the Oval Office—but like his homie Doctor Dre, Beck's still got love for the street. Word."[124]

The intro to "Get Real Paid" is supposed to imitate the sound of robots fucking, taking Beck's Kraftwerk infatuation to another level. This is the blue-eyed nu skool of hip-hop circa 2023, with its herky-jerky beats and disembodied space-age rip-rapping: "We like the girls/With the cellophane chests." Peering over the fence of Paisley Park for inspiration, "Peaches & Cream" is Beck's unabashed tribute to Prince (who wrote a pair of tunes entitled "Peach" and "Cream" respectively).

Originally entitled "Out of Kontrol," "Broken Train" garnered a name change when a song entitled "Out of Control" was discovered on the Chemical Brothers's *Surrender* album. The tune's casual beat is reminiscent of "Jack-Ass" and "Deadweight," but the Ohio Players-esque guitar squawk and harmonica jives enliven the song's energy level.

Ex-Smiths guitarist Johnny Marr lends a hand on the swooning outro of "Milk & Honey" and, though he reportedly recorded guitar for another song entitled "The Doctor," these are the only Marr licks that make it on the finished product. The tune embodies a portion of Buzz Clifford's "I See I Am," so Beck shares writing credit for this fuzzy slab of rocked-out funk and sleazy electronicapop.

U.K. neo-folk chanteuse Beth Orton lent backing vox for "Beautiful Way." Beck's and Beth's voices come together in a harmonious understatement as lap steel guitarists Jay Dee Maness (the Carpenters, the Byrds, Lyle Lovett) and Greg Leisz weave an atmospheric backdrop. The last song from the Beck-produced sessions, "Pressure Zone," sounds like a mix between Blur's "Song 2" and a Devo riff. Rocking as much as it rolls, the tune gives rise to one of Beck's most touching lyrics: "I could sleep inside her bones/A hundred years."

Beck had opted to coproduce two ditties with the Dust Brothers at PCP Labs. The Atari beatbox hip-hop of "Hollywood Freaks" is Beck's half-serious, half-joking tribute to the sounds of the streets, which he cowrote with Simpson and King. The tune had the setlist title "Jockin' My Mercedes" during the 1998 shows—taken from the line "Jockin' my Mercedes/Probably have my baby." The other collaborative effort was the album-closing epic "Debra," the tune formerly known as "I Wanna Get With You (and Your Sister Debra)," and perhaps the most soulful slice of preacherman balladry Beck had ever laid down on tape. Beck, the Dust Brothers, and Ed Greene all get writing credit, because the melody was nicked from the latter's "My Love for You," made popular by Ramsey Lewis. "Debra" exemplifies the boundaries Beck was pushing with his voice by incorporating shrill falsettos, sultry growls, and over-the-top shrieks. For the first time, Beck was full-on singing in a manner that would make Marvin Gaye, Prince, *and* Freddie Mercury proud.

This foray into Motown madness is Momus's favorite Beck track to date, as he explains: "I love the perverse way he takes the conventions of a genre which is just about straightforward hedonism—rap, R&B—and makes them sound alien, decadent, otherworldly. It's a bit like what Bowie did when he invented Plastic Soul. There's a heightened sense of evil that runs through all Beck's songs, a sensitivity to moral pollution which only someone with rather high personal moral standards would have. I can totally 'smell the VD in the club tonite' when I listen to this song, and yet it's weary and strange and beautiful too. This song's ass is in the gutter, but its eyes are on Venus."[125]

"It's humorous, and I was afraid of that. I thought people would think it was making fun of the genre,"[126] Beck told *Rolling Stone*. Instead of mocking the form, though, the song glorifies it by paying homage in its grandiose manner. "Debra" exemplifies Beck's passion for R&B and BET's current playlist of wannabe Don Juans and overstated smooth criminals.

> I love the cheesiness, and the sexuality is just so uninhibited
> and has a playfulness and a humor to it. It's so straight out but
> it's also coupled with little bits of sincerity: "Ooh I love you."
> These guys are crying! In the rock world, you're not really allowed
> to explore that more vulnerable side of masculinity, so I got
> really interested in that. I was really tired of the rock posturing

of the grunge era and the openness of R&B was really refreshing to me: "I wanna lick you up and down and make your body real hot."[127]

Indeed, the sexuality of R&B music is clearly a style Beck is trying to emulate over the entire breadth of *Midnite Vultures*. "In R&B, you can have a love song that has layers," he says. "It can be real and true and deep, but it can also be playful. It can be unabashedly sexual in a way that would come off as trite in a rock song. The main attraction is the possibility for ambiguity. You can have unrequited love and full-blown lust. You can have a sense of humor, but that doesn't mean it's not deep. I don't think anywhere else in American culture you get that."[128] This insightful comment harkens back to Beck's interview of Tom Petty for *Musician* when Petty wryly noted, "R&B videos are very interesting now. I notice that there's a lot of people with ski lodges." "Ski lodges and a barbecue," Beck affirmed, then continued. "Well, it's all fantasy. That's what you get when you win the lottery or something." "Yeah, you get a ski lodge with twenty girls in bikinis,"[129] Petty jokingly finishes.

Looking at *Midnite Vultures's* overarching themes and philosophies, one finds that the collection serves as Beck's vivisection of sexual mores and their presentation in popular media. It was the most overtly "sexual" project he had ever embarked upon. Typical of Beck is his atypical angle of perception of the MTV generation's coming-of-age odyssey. When he sings, "I'll leave graffiti/Where you've never been kissed" on "Nicotine & Gravy," it's a statement of his unorthodox probings into the usually overblown and overglamorized world of sexual politics.

After the last take of the last track was in the can, the record was mixed by various combinations of Beck, Tony Hoffer, Mickey Petralia, and hip-hop mixing maestro Michael Patterson (who has worked on some of the biggest urban records ever, including the Notorius B.I.G.'s *Life After Death,* Puff Daddy's *No Way Out,* R. Kelly's *R.,* and L.L. Cool J's *Phenomenon*). Patterson was a very conscientious choice for Beck, who wanted to incorporate a more hip-hop flavor in his work, as he told *Vibe:* "I have strong memories of hip-hop being a force in my life from an early age," he remembered. "It was the thing that pulled everyone together on the bus to school. You had all combinations of people listening to it."[130] He later noted, "Rap is a distinct place between speech and song. I used to feel constricted by song structures, melody structures. There are certain things you can say in a rap that would never sound good in a melody. I felt like by rapping I was free to say all kinds of things."[131]

Despite the change in musical direction, the album's lyrics remain as scattered and nebulous as ever, pulling in phraseology and references from several alien cultures that only Beck seems to have contact with. From "Midnight hags in the mausoleum/Where the pixilated doctors moan" to "Hot milk/Mmmm . . . tweak my nipple," Beck never fails to confound, confuse, and randomly delight with his po-mo poetry. When confronted by an English journo as to how deep his lyrics could possibly be and whether he's exposing any true part of himself, Beck quickly replied:

> Oh yeah! That's all I do. I can pull out my lyrics and say: "That's me. I couldn't dig any deeper to get that out." I mean, I could say, "I wish we could still be friends" and shit like that, because I have those emotions. But I would rather say, "I'll be your chauffeur on a midnight drive/It takes a miracle just to survive/Buried animals call your name." Because to me those lyrics call up such a huge thread of my experience. Maybe it's not quite as acceptable to use that type of language to express things. I could go in and say something very generic and perfunctory, and people might think that's a nice simulation of my emotional landscape. There is all this emotional language that we're conditioned to think is meaningful, but I would argue that only a few people are able to create, with simple language, really affecting lyrics that connect with people's emotional core. I have to find other sorts of language to communicate where my mind is at."[132]

When further prodded about the lyric he just mentioned, Beck help-lessly says:

> Well I can tell you five things that that means to me. But I understand. My own girlfriend's always giving me shit about this. She's like, "Why don't you just say what you mean?" But most of the time that's how I express myself. I don't think I would have gotten a tenth as far as I have if it was just clever wordplay thrown in with a bunch of cool sounds. People wouldn't have responded to it. I feel like I do strive to come up with the most simple thing, but it's got to have me in it. Otherwise it just feels generic. It's not that I'm using things to hide behind, but who says you're not allowed to open the palate of imagery and words? I don't understand who wrote these rules of what's acceptable and what's right. I hate that.[133]

Musing on *Midnite Vultures* as an artistic whole, Beck measured it against the cultural climate it was emerging in:

> I think it's more the period. This point in time seems more power-oriented. Power workout, power diet, power body parts, power relationships, power steering, *Power Rangers*. People are scrubbed and clean, well toned and manicured. I recently saw *The Last American Virgin,* one of those early-'80s coming-of-age movies. And the actors, they look like kids you grew up with! Today's teen movies, I didn't know anybody who looked like that. The standards now are so unbelievably high.[134]

CHAPTER 8

The Culture Vulture Descends

"Sleep on a bus is never restful. The continual jostling of the road and hum of the engine keeps one in a state of half-sleep and weary semiconsciousness. It's a very specific kind of sleep. If you look into the eyes of a touring musician, you can see that look, which only comes from having slept on buses for months on end. There is a tacit sympathy between those who recognize that look in each other's eyes. It is a look of imminent maniacal laughter and abject resignation."

To increase prerelease fervor for *Midnite Vultures,* Beck played a trio of October shows. There were two college dates before headlining the second night of the Coachella Music and Art Festival alongside Morrissey, Tool, Rage Against the Machine, Chemical Brothers, Jurassic 5, and Ben Harper. This good-vibes celebration was in sharp contrast to the riots and disastrous results of that year's Woodstock, and Beck used this backdrop to debut a majority of the new album. The press did their part to pump the

Beck does *Total Request Live*. PHOTO COURTESY OF SCOTT GRIES/IMAGEDIRECT

release—*SPIN's* September 1999 cover boasted a shot of Beck alongside pictures of Lauryn Hill, Trent Reznor, and the late Kurt Cobain with the headline, "The 90 Greatest Albums of the '90s."

Geffen execs decided that "Sexx Laws" would be the best way to introduce the collection to the listening public, and the video debuted on MTV's *Total Request Live* on November 3. Three days later, Beck made a point to stop by the studios to talk about directing the video and to perform for bland-man host Carson Daly and the Times Square pop junkies. Complete with band, Beck blasted through a truly inspired version of the single, transforming his three and a half minutes into a symphonic melee of struts, splits, and stances. The video itself features Jack Black (actor and singer of Tenacious D) as the main character alongside a variety of demonically possessed household appliances (recalling the in-studio mayhem when recording "Cancelled Check"). Unfortunately, the song and video were a little too cutting edge for the teeny-boppers infatuated with Britneys, Bizkits, and Backstreets, and it quickly fell off the *TRL* charts.

Not betting the bank on *TRL* to solely sell the record, Geffen booked a bevy of other television appearances to support the single both Stateside and abroad. In the U.K., Beck performed the song on *Top of the Pops* on November 12 next to Jennifer Lopez, the Spice Girls, and Savage Garden, and again on November 18 for the music-video show *Videotech*. Finally, he dropped by *Later With Jools Holland* to perform a trio of tunes for the British pop icon. Back on home turf, he stopped by the NBC studios on December 4 as the musical guest of *Saturday Night Live,* where he funked, rattled, and rolled through "Sexx Laws" and "Mixed Bizness." The next day he hawked his wares at the VH1/Vogue Fashion Awards at New York City's Armory, a show hosted by the ubiquitous P. Diddy and Heather Locklear. Now a card-carrying fashionista, Beck's new look for *Midnite Vultures* was a combination of eighties retro and casual indie attire that highlighted his lanky frame and ever-youthful face. To round out his public appearances, Beck played *The Tonight Show with Jay Leno* to get on the airwaves and boast his new look one last time before Christmas.

Unfortunately, no amount of promo made that somewhat disconcerting single a hit in the States. It had a disappointing shelf life on radio, only hitting #21 on *Billboard's* Modern Rock Tracks chart. However, when "Sexx Laws" was released on October 25 in the U.K. as a two-part single, it managed to crack their Top 40. The U.K. offices included a bevy of bonus tracks on the singles: the turntable-scratched eighties-vibed "This Is My Crew," "Sexx Laws (Wiseguys Remix)," "Salt in the Wound" (which veers between an opening riff from the Stooges's "I Wanna Be Your Dog" and general funkiness), and "Sexx Laws (Malibu Mix)," which was remixed by Roger Manning. Elsewhere in the world the song was well received, making a good showing on the German, Australian, New Zealand, and Japanese charts.

Beck plays the VH1 Fashion Awards. PHOTO COURTESY OF SCOTT GRIES/IMAGEDIRECT

With the first single faltering on radio and TV, *Midnite Vultures* was released November 23, 1999, debuting at a somewhat disappointing #34 on the *Billboard* charts. This placing left the pundits, who had seen the early nineties alt-rawk movement go the way of the dodo, wondering whether Beck could still survive in the pop and rap-metal marketplace.

Though the sales weren't immediately there, the majority of the reviews glowed like a Chernobyl Christmas tree. *Newsweek* wrote, "For all his cutting-edginess, Beck is a throwback to the days before LPs. Each track here is a record in itself, with an almost Ellington-ian wealth of detail, color, and texture."[135] He graced the November cover of *SPIN*, dubbed the "Funk Soul Brother," and the enclosed feature brims with praise for the newest collection, declaring it "a giddy pimp-roll through boulevard funk, sci-fi hip-hop, and late-century R&B."[136]

However, these positive reviews were offset by several key critics who were somewhat confounded by Beck's new direction. Ethan Smith of *New York* commented, "Too gifted a performer not to be entertaining but too smart to ever entertain solely at face value, Beck seems to embrace his stardom while deconstructing it. His interest in urban music styles—especially the over-the-top soul that inspired 'Debra' (think Philip Bailey's delivery on 'Reasons')—seems to be genuine, but it's hardly straightforward or, often, sincere."[137] *Time Out New York* couldn't decide either: "In a pop moment when even Axl Rose promises his band's new album will be a 'melting pot' of sounds, it's probably too much to ask *Midnite Vultures* to pack the unique, bric-a-brac punch of *Odelay*. I think it's almost his best album; others are going to like it a lot (while probably suffering from a bit of familiarity-breeds-contempt syndrome). And, of course, Ween fans will consider it another sham from the greatest bullshit artist of the decade."[138]

Waffling aside, *Midnite Vultures* ended up on some prestigious roll calls as per usual. *Q* magazine ranked it in its "50 Best Albums of 1999," *Mojo* ranked it #8 in their "Best of 1999," and *CMJ* placed it at #21 in their "Top 30 Editorial Picks." Immediately following the Christmas buying rush, *Midnite Vultures* staggered into gold and would later sell close to a million copies on American soil.

Strike a pose. PHOTO COURTESY OF SCOTT GRIES/IMAGEDIRECT

Preaching to the converted. PHOTO COURTESY OF SCOTT J. HURTWITZ, 2001

With the exception of some preholiday one-offs, including a December 3 stop in Philly at the Y-100 Festival with Moby, Oasis, and the Foo Fighters, Beck stayed below the radar. He spent nine days in January shooting Steve Hanft's film, *Southlander* (it had been originally titled *Recycler),* in which he plays himself ten years in the future, alongside Beth Orton, Elliott Smith, and Hank Williams III. *Southlander* follows a guy named Chance searching for his long-lost Moletron synthesizer. If there's a modern love story, this is it.

The first leg of the U.S. *Midnite Vultures* tour ran from January 25 in Austin, Texas, at the Music Hall, to February 19 at the Patriot Center in Washington, D.C. Translating the complex and sweeping album into a live setting was a daunting task, but Beck's ten-piece band was ready for it. In anticipation of the tour, Beck talked about his verve for playing live: "I love the kind of abandon that you feel onstage when your own will has been removed and you are completely vulnerable and no longer in control. You may look vulnerable. You may even look idiotic, but there's something honest and revealing going on."[139]

The setlist consisted of "Mixed Bizness," "Novacane," "The New Pollution," "Nicotine & Gravy," "Pressure Zone," "Loser," "Deadweight," "Milk & Honey," "Debra," "Hollywood Freaks," "Peaches & Cream," "Jack-Ass," and "Where It's At." DJ Swamp returned to the stage solely to warm up the crowd before the encore by scratching the Kingsmen's lone hit "Louie Louie" and Deep Purple's "Smoke on the Water." When the full ensemble assembles again, they romp through "Sexx Laws" and "Devils Haircut" before calling it a wrap. *The All-Star News* gushed: "Fully Y2K compliant, Mr. Hansen's soul revue appropriated the old-school sci-fi props of Parliament/Funkadelic, and cut a swath through Beck's hit catalogue while sampling heavily from his latest album. With giant light sticks floating above the stage, three horn players, two backup singers, and a giant disco ball, the fireworks this night left the band's recent television appearances in the dust."[140]

The composition of the setlist remained essentially the same throughout the tour, though the order of the songs constantly changed. For the most part, Beck stuck to the material from *Midnite Vultures*, adding various older tracks to keep it interesting and appease fans. Occasionally he took a moment to do a solo acoustic number, usually choosing a *Mutations* tune as his muse.

Let's take a minute to introduce the band. On guitar—Lyle Workman (Frank Black, Todd Rundgren, Jellyfish). On bass—the incomparable Justin Meldal-Johnsen. On keyboards—the one and only Roger Joseph Manning Jr. Ladies and gentlemen, please give a warm welcome to drummer Victor Indrizzo (Redd Kross, Depeche Mode, Scott Weiland). And turn your attention to the turntables, folks—DJ Swamp (remixer of the Cardigans, Morcheeba and the Bloodhound Gang). The brass menagerie features David Brown on alto sax, David Ralicke on baritone saxophone and trombone, and Jon Birdsong on trumpet. Last but not least, let's hear it for the loveliest backup singers in the business—Glenys Rogers and Johari Funches-Penny.

For openers on the U.S. jaunt, Beck brought along Hank Williams III for the first half and Beth Orton to finish out the second half. During his second night headlining Radio City Music Hall in New York, he invited Orton onstage to do an acoustic version of the Stones's "No Expectations" from their classic 1968 offering *Beggar's Banquet*. The night after, he performed "Sexx Laws" at the American Music Awards before finishing out the last two dates of the tour.

In early January, two huge nominations were announced. The Brit Awards (the U.K. equivalent of the Grammys) gave a nod to Beck in their Best International Male Solo Artist category, an award he would walk away with for his third year in a row. Perhaps more importantly, however, *Mutations* had been nominated for a Best Alternative Performance Grammy. Though Elton John referred to the Grammys that year as "mostly bullshit," Beck reeled in another gold gramophone for his work.

At the end of February, the Stephane Sednaoui–directed vid for "Mixed Bizness" debuted on MTV. Sednaoui's articulate and discerning eye has been responsible for a number of genre-defining MTV clips, including Red Hot Chili Peppers's "Give It Away," U2's "Mysterious Ways," Smashing Pumpkins's "Today," and Alanis Morissette's naked romp "Thank U." Beck had never embraced a straightforward video premise, and this disorienting clip, flickering between hypercolored disco-styled footage and black-and-white beach scenes, is no more "normal" than the rest. For this particular video, we find Beck peering through a telescope while bikini-clad girls dance about with sharks on their heads. Despite a costly budget and a funky hook, the track only hit #36 on *Billboard's* Modern Rock Tracks chart in March of the new millennium and failed to make a dent with the MTV viewership.

In the U.K., however, the single found a much more appreciative audience. Geffen U.K. issued it as a two-part single featuring remixes of the title track by Cornelius, DJ Me DJ You, and Les Rythmes Digitales, an unheard gem entitled "Dirty, Dirty," and bonus CD-ROM content of the video for the A-side as well as for "Sexx Laws." To seize the PR moment, Beck headed to England to perform on *Top of the Pops* alongside the Spice Girls, Savage Garden, and the suddenly ubiquitous Santana.

With the Anglophiles conquered, Beck spent all of March zigzagging his way across Europe, bringing his unparalleled revue to zealous fans. Sometimes it was Beck himself who got caught up in the feverish passion of the

The boy with faraway eyes. PHOTO COURTESY OF SCOTT GRIES/IMAGEDIRECT

moment. On March 23, he was hospitalized after impaling himself on the end of a bass guitar during the encore of "Devils Haircut" at London's Wembley Arena. He was released after doctors confirmed he had only fallen prey to some "deep internal bruising."

During the course of the U.S. leg, Beck posted a diary entry to msn.com. It was a brief depiction of road burnout and relentless touring that sounds like something Hunter S. Thompson would have written if he had gone on to be a roadie for the Allman Brothers:

> I was trying to adjust to the hustle and activity all around. We were all groggy and slow, collecting ourselves in the lobby. Though we'd slept all night, it wasn't restful. Sleep on a bus is never restful. The continual jostling of the road and hum of the engine keeps one in a state of half-sleep and weary semiconsciousness. It's a very specific kind of sleep. If you look into the eyes of a touring musician, you can see that look, which only comes from having slept on buses for months on end. There Is a tacit sympathy between those who recognize that look in each other's eyes. It is a look of imminent maniacal laughter and abject resignation."[141]

Returning to the homeland, Beck performed the little-known Cymande song "Bra" with the percussion groove collective Ozomatli at the Fifth Annual ALMA Awards on April 15. To finish up his televised obligations, Beck knocked out four tunes for an episode of *Doug and Jimmy's Farmclub* and appeared in a *Behind the Music 2* on VH1. In late April and early May, Beck swept through the Southwest and West Coast before climbing on a big jet plane for a nine-date Japanese jaunt.

After this nonstop, world-hopping tour, Beck took the next two months off with a couple of notable exceptions. On June 16, Beck performed for a hometown crowd at Largo along with Justin, Roger, and host/producer Jon Brion (Fiona Apple, Aimee Mann) on the *Jon Brion and Friends* weekly radio program.

The foursome ripped through a grungy medley (Alice in Chains's "Rooster," Pearl Jam's "Even Flow," Stone Temple Pilots's "Wicked Garden," and Soundgarden's "Blackhole Sun"), two new songs, and an acoustic version of "Sexx Laws." Later that month, Beck coheadlined the Sweet Relief Musician's Fund's Annual Medicine Ball with Patti Smith on June 20 in Los Angeles. His half-hour, seven-song solo set included "Sing It Again" and "Dead Melodies" from *Mutations*, as well as a cover of "John Hardy," an old folk song popularized by Leadbelly.

He rejoined the rest of his band to kick out the jams at the Experience Music Project in Seattle on June 24. It was a "greatest hits" set, opening with a shortened version of "Loser" and closing with his cover of Eddy Grant's 1982 hit "Electric Avenue." Swinging back to the hometown crowd, Beck scooped the ribbon for Best Rock/Pop Songwriter/Composer at the *L.A. Weekly* Music Awards 2000 on June 29 alongside a variety of locals and well-known national acts, including Rage Against the Machine, Macy Gray, and the eels.

Back in full-band mode, the collective swooped the headlining slot of the This Ain't No Picnic Festival in Irvine, California, at the Oak Canyon Ranch on Sunday, July 2. Joined by the likes of Built to Spill, Creeper Lagoon, Yo La Tengo, At the Drive-In, and remix cohort DJ Me DJ You, Beck and company played a stunning, hour-long, acoustic-oriented gig. The five-thousand-strong crowd of fey indie kids got a diverse setlist, including older material from *One Foot in the Grave*, a coked-up version of "Devils Haircut," and a few *Mutations* tunes.

Soon thereafter, Beck threw an extravagant b-day bash at Micheltorena Mansion, a converted monastery in the Silverlake hills. Elliott Smith, Perry Farrell, and Exene Cervenka cavorted about in the absence of Beck's longtime flame Leigh Limon, with whom he had broken up three weeks prior. Word on the street later had it that Beck was doin' the nasty with Winona Ryder, a fact that Michael Krugman and Jason Cohen didn't miss in their weekly column "Well Hung at Dawn" on *Rollingstone.com*. "Did you hear that Beck's dating Winona Ryder? Doesn't he know she's the kiss of death? She's rock's greatest career killer, though *Midnite Vultures* may well have done the job regardless."[142] Doh! However, things seemed to have cooled off by the Thanksgiving season when the pair downsized their relationship to friendship status.

Beck can't get no satisfaction. PHOTO COURTESY OF SCOTT GRIES/IMAGEDIRECT

Sleazy Hollywood relationships aside, summer 2000 was a time for Beck fans to purchase a few extra collectibles for their collections. The *Free Tibet* DVD included Beck performing "Asshole" and "One Foot in the Grave" at the 1996 Tibetan Freedom Concert at San Francisco's Golden Gate Park. The Japanese branch of Geffen was busy pressing up an eight-song B-side collection entitled *Stray Blues* that packaged together some of the outstanding flipsides of Beck's singles. Beck aficionados also spent some time tracking down issues of *Glue* magazine that included "American Car," which was recorded by Bean during the time Beck had briefly joined their lineup. To round out the collector's corner, *Farm Aid Volume 1* featured Beck and Willie Nelson's duet of "Peach Pickin' Time in Georgia," and Beck was called in to remix David Bowie's new single, "Seven," taken from his latest outing, *hours....*

At the end of July, Beck brought his traveling circus to festivals and venues across Europe, finishing up at the Reading Festival in England. To coincide with the tour, he released a European-only single for "Nicotine & Gravy" that came with two bonus tracks, "Midnite Vultures" and "Zatyricon" (a hilarious track which features producer Tony Hoffer making a prank call to a cosmetic surgery clinic inquiring about various odd procedures), as well as the enhanced bonus video for the A-side. The European shows were a true triumph for Beck. Though the album wasn't performing as well as hoped in the States, the Eurokids were eating up his every utterance, and he was one of the most critically praised acts on the festival circuit.

After some long-deserved R and R in the fall, Beck engaged in some sporadic gigs as a final promotional push for his most recent product. He and the full band headlined the Now and Zen Fest for San Fran's Alice Radio in Golden Gate Park along with the eclectic likes of Travis, the Go-Go's, Tonic, and Keanu Reeves's lesser known pastime, Dogstar. Then, as a solo acoustic act, he opened five Neil Young dates and played a pair of gigs at L.A.'s Wiltern Theatre.

Despite his irregular touring schedule, Beck kept popping up in the L.A. area to pay tribute to some of his favorite charities. With only his acoustic guitar in tow at the fourteenth annual Bridge School Benefit with Tom Petty and the Heartbreakers, the Foo Fighters, and Red Hot Chili Peppers, Beck performed a cover of Hank Williams and Jimmie Davis's "(I Heard That) Lonesome Whistle" and an *espagnol* version of "Jack-Ass." He played the Silver Lining Benefit for the Hollywood Sunset Free Clinic at the Paramour Estate in Los Angeles on November 4, along with Rufus Wainwright and Aimee Mann. Beck regaled the crowd with some rarely heard covers, including John Martyn's "Go Easy" and Daniel Johnston's "Some Things Last a Long Time," before closing out his set with "Nobody's Fault But My Own." To round out his charitable performances, Beck stopped by Hollywood's Knitting Factory to raise money for that dog's Petra Hayden, who was in a car accident in August and, lacking medical insurance, had racked up a hundred-thousand-dollar hospital bill. Victoria Williams, Tenacious D, and the Go-Go's, with various singers at the helm—including Beck and Matthew Sweet—rounded out the evening. Beck's solo set stuck to the old reliables, though he did throw in a rendition of George Jones's "She Still Thinks I Care" for the country-crooning fans in the audience.

In September, Beck headed into the studio with rap producer Timbaland to work on material for the both of them. The unlikely twosome met during a U.S. TV show taping in the spring and had been intent on the idea of a collaboration ever since. According to the *NME,* Timbaland said, "We were talking about doing a song for each other, and we made it happen. That's basically how that happened. Most people talk about it, but then they don't pursue it. This one we tried to pursue."[143] The first fruits of these labors was Beck's cover of David Bowie's "Diamond Dogs" for the soundtrack to the Baz Luhrman flick *Moulin Rouge.* He joked about the version with *RollingStone.com:* "We gotta put some ghetto-tech in there, because we heard that was the next big thing. We're going to ride the ghetto-tech wave to the next Grammys."[144] During the same sessions, Beck lent his vox to a song tentatively entitled "Our Music" for Aaliyah's next album that Timbaland is in the midst of producing.

Despite the fact that Beck failed to win any VH1 Music Awards in November, he unexpectedly garnered two Grammy nods for Best Album and Best Alternative Album in January. "Someone called and woke me up and I think I yelled, like a decrepit old cowboy, *'Aaagh-ooh-hoo'!'*" Beck recounted. "I didn't anticipate it, I never anticipate anything, and I certainly wasn't anticipating even anticipating. But it was sweet, a nice validation, since I worked insanely hard on this last one. And then I thought, it was kind of weird, like it fit in between times. It's really a 2000 record, though it came out at the end of 1999. It was built for 2000, like a car model that comes out just a little before."[145] The night of the Grammys, however, Beck lost Best Album to unlikely stars of the evening Steely Dan and Best Alternative Album to Radiohead's much-hyped *Kid A.*

Beck's first gig of 2001 was the Rock in Rio for a Better World festival in Rio de Janeiro at the end of January. The international side of the lineup pulled together perhaps the most diverse group of pop stars ever as Sheryl Crow, R.E.M., Foo Fighters, 'NSYNC, Britney Spears, Red Hot Chili Peppers, Iron Maiden, James Taylor, and Rob Halford all graced the same stage. In his write-up of the review for *CDNow.com,* Kevin Raub joked "Beck . . . pulled back some-what on his usual stage banter during his twelve-song set, perhaps due to the fact that much of his humor would be lost on the Brazilians (Hell, it's some-times lost on Americans!)."[146]

His first TV appearance that year was on February 1, gracing Jay Leno's stage to perform a funked-up version of "Nicotine & Gravy." According to his publicist, Beck was involved in working on his next opus. "He's got absolutely loads of songs recorded already, but we'll have to see what happens."[147] With that being said, thus closes another chapter in the Beck story.

CHAPTER 9

Future Pollution

"[ ] have a record of solo acoustic fingerpicking songs that I've been working on for ten years," Beck told *RollingStone.com*. "Then I have an obnoxious rock record I've recorded, and there's a record I want to make with Kool Keith that we've finished three tracks for. I'd also like to do a covers album. Then, my favorite thing is to just go into a studio with nothing in my head and see what comes out."[148] When talking to the *L.A. Weekly,* he was just as indecisive: "I have a whole other album's worth of songs we recorded for *[Midnite Vultures].* I also have several tracks I've been working on with the Dust Brothers over the last two years, and we still have unreleased stuff from *Odelay* in the can. I want to do an album in Spanish, and I've wanted to go to Nashville and do a straight country record since I first picked up a guitar."[149] None of this truly sheds any light on the direction of Beck's new album, but at least it will definitely goad the fires of speculation in the meantime.

For the true Beck fanatic, there are all sorts of rarities floating around on Napster and elsewhere—tracks recorded during various album sessions that didn't make the final cut, rare foreign B-sides, demos, home-recorded tracks from the earlier portion of Beck's career, and a slew of live cuts. Despite the availability of the material (albeit illegally), it is oftentimes poorly recorded, incorrectly labeled, or just plain hard to track down.

Since the thin man lacks a full-on live release (limiting his live tracks to a few compilation contributions, including *Bridge School Concert Volume 1* and *SNL 25: Saturday Night Live Musical Performance Volume 2)*, one with the entire band or just the acoustic guitar would appease a long-voiced fan desire.

There are several unreleased tracks fans are most eager to hear, including Beck's cover of Can's "I'm So Green" and his remix of Digital Underground's seminal booty anthem "Humpty Dance." Confirmed releases for the future include the pair of tunes on Air's new album, *10,000 Hz Legend*, on which Beck lent his distinctive vox. He has recorded a cover of "Stagger Lee" for a forthcoming Mississippi John Hurt tribute record, as well as a cover of

"(I Heard That) Lonesome Whistle Blow" for a Hank Williams tribute that is in the works. Finally, Beck has been working with Marianne Faithfull on material for her new album, and it is rumored that he has sung on at least two tracks.

Steve Hanft has supposedly been working on a tour video tentatively entitled *Computer Chips and Salsa* since 1998. Though he gathered footage at a quartet of shows during the *Odelay* tour and has spoken publicly about it, there is no set release date.

Needless to say, there are many compositions that remain on heavily guarded tape reels in a record label vault which we know nothing about. Even more intriguing are the songs in Beck's head that he has yet to lay to tape in any form and remain unrealized, intangible concepts. Beck has a seemingly endless wealth of material that doesn't want to stop expanding. Attempting to gather it all will provide many long, yet entertaining, hours of searching for diehard fans the world over.

o Just Let the Tape Run Out...

ometimes in a private haze, with the stereo running steady and the lights way down, you float back to the first time you encountered a particular song. In college, I would religiously watch pre-Pinfield indie icon Lewis Largent on MTV's *120 Minutes* while slurping down Napoli's pizza and desperately trying to persuade myself that I didn't have a massive paper due the next day. Pavement's "Cut Your Hair," Smashing Pumpkins's "Today," and Suede's "Animal Nitrate" were my classics. One night, amid the grunge poseurs, Britpoppers, punk rocketeers, and indie meanderings, Beck's "Loser" crash-landed and became permanently etched into my THC-ridden skull.

A few more albums down the pike, and Beck still confounds me as much as he entertains me. When I first saw him play "Debra" live, with all its beguiling R&B shrills and crescendos, I was lost in the beautiful moment and utterly converted all over again. There are only a handful of artists in mainstream music that have as much leeway and creativity as Beck. With each new step he takes, we sit, wide-eyed and bedazzled, not totally sure what to make of this spectacle. Even when we expect the unexpected, we are astonished at the results. As far a cry from the prototypical "rock star" as one could imagine, Beck operates as the inside outsider, creating his own rules and living his own game. He is, without a doubt, one of the most inspired artists of our time.

With a growing legacy already behind him and the whole future before him, Beck knows how important a role he will play. "Our lifestyles now, we don't get to escape to a beautiful meadow, or some lakeside beautiful spot. We need music or movies to get out of the drudgery or the pressure, the stress of our environment. We live in these incredibly unnatural environments—unnatural in the sense that they're completely different than what's preceded it for the last ten thousand years. So music is important. It's a physical thing."[150]

Who really knows what will be next for Beck? Not me, not you, maybe not even Beck. So have a smoke, sit back, and relax—we've got a long ride ahead of us.

PHOTO COURTESY OF SCOTT GRIES/IMAGEDIRECT

FULL LENGTHERS

Golden Feelings
Released by Sonic Enemy, 1993

The Fucked Up Blues
Special People
Magic Station Wagon
No Money No Honey
Trouble All My Days
Feeling Hurter
Bad Energy
Schmoozer
Heartland Feeling
Super Golden Black Sunchild
Soul Sucked Dry
Feelings
Gettin' Home
Will I Be Ignored by the Lord
Bogus Soul
Totally Confused
Mutherfukka
People Gettin Busy

Released again in a limited run in 1999.

A Western Harvest Field by Moonlight
Released by Fingerpaint Records, 1994

Totally Confused
Mayonaise Salad
Gettin Home
Blackfire Choked Our Death
Feel Like a Piece of Shit (Mind Control)
She Is All (Gimme Something to Eat)
Pinefresh
Lampshade
Feel Like a Piece of Shit (Crossover Potential)
Mango Vader Rocks!
Feel Like a Piece of Shit (Cheetoes Time)
Styrofoam Chicken (Quality Time)

Original pressing of 3,000 10-inchers came with miniature fingerpaintings made by Beck and friends at the record release party. The album has been re-pressed three times over the years; however, it is currently out of print.

Stereopathetic Soul Manure
Released by Gusto Productions/Flipside Records, February 22, 1994

Pink Noise (Rock Me Amadeus)
Rowboat
Thunder Peel
Waitin' for a Train
The Spirit Moves Me
Crystal Clear (Beer)
No Money No Honey
8.6.82
Total Soul Future (Eat It)
One Foot in the Grave
Aphid Manure Heist
Today Has Been a Fucked Up Day
"Rollins Power Sauce"
Puttin It Down
11.6.45

Cut 1/2 Blues
Jagermeister Pie
Ozzy
Dead Wild Cat
Satan Gave Me a Taco
8.4.82
Tasergun
Modesto

Various pressings of this disc come with "End-of-Disc-Bonus-Noise-Galore."

Mellow Gold
Released by DGC/Bong Load Custom Records, March 1, 1994

Loser
Pay No Mind (Snoozer)
Fuckin With My Head (Mountain Dew Rock)
Whiskeyclone, Hotel City 1997
Soul Suckin Jerk
Truckdrivin Neighbors Downstairs (Yellow Sweat)
Sweet Sunshine
Beercan
Steal My Body Home
Nitemare Hippy Girl
Mutherfuker
Blackhole

The Australian version initially came packaged with a tour sampler that included "Mexico," "Totally Confused," "Jagermeister Pie," "Lampshade," and "Rowboat."

One Foot in the Grave
Released by K Records, June 27, 1994

He's a Mighty Good Leader
Sleeping Bag
I Get Lonesome
Burnt Orange Peel
Cyanide Breath Mint
See Water

Ziplock Bag
Hollow Log
Forcefield
Fourteen Rivers Fourteen Floods
Asshole
I've Seen the Land Beyond
Outcome
Girl Dreams
Painted Eyelids
Atmospheric Conditions

The Japanese version comes with the three tracks found on the "It's All in Your Mind" 7-inch, the title track, "Feather in Your Cap," and "Whiskey Can Can."

Odelay
Released by DGC/Bong Load Custom Records, June 18, 1996

Devils Haircut
Hotwax
Lord Only Knows
The New Pollution
Derelict
Novacane
Jack-Ass
Where It's At
Minus
Sissyneck
Readymade
High 5 (Rock the Catskills)
Ramshackle

The U.K. version comes with a bonus track, "Diskobox," produced by Jon Spencer. A limited edition U.K. version of the album finds the unlisted bonus track "Clock" attached as well. In the land Down Under, the label packaged it with a cool tour sampler that was the "Sissyneck" single, which included the title track, "Burro" (Mariachi version of the title track), "Dark and Lovely" (remix by Dust Brothers), "Devil Got My Woman," and "Brother."

Mutations
Released by DGC/Bong Load Custom Records, November 3, 1998

Cold Brains
Nobody's Fault But My Own
Lazy Flies
Canceled Check
We Live Again
Tropicalia
Dead Melodies
Bottle of Blues
O Maria
Sing It Again
Static

There is an unlisted track, "Diamond Bollocks," on the regular CD release; the vinyl version finds that song as well as "Runners Dial Zero" included on a bonus 7-inch. The U.K. CD version comes with "Runners Dial Zero" as an added extra for fans, and the German version packages both the aforementioned tracks as well as the bonus B-sides from the U.K. "Tropicalia" single, "Halo of Gold," and "Black Balloon." To further complicate matters for picky collectors, the Japanese version included "Electric Music and the Summer People" that was recorded during the *Odelay* sessions, as well as both "Diamond Bollocks" and "Runners Dial Zero." Australia chose to keep the same tracklisting as the U.S. vinyl for their CD release.

Midnite Vultures
Released by DGC Records, November 23, 1999

Sexx Laws
Nicotine & Gravy
Mixed Bizness
Get Real Paid
Hollywood Freaks
Peaches & Cream
Broken Train
Milk & Honey
Beautiful Way
Pressure Zone
Debra

The first half-million copies of the U.S. release came in a unique digipak format. Best Buy customers got a bonus disc with three songs from the U.K. "Sexx Laws" single release—"Salt in the Wound," "This Is My Crew," and "Sexx Laws (Malibu Mix by Roger Manning)." Meanwhile, the Japanese added one bonus song, "Arabian Nights," to their version of the release.

Stray Blues: A Collection of B-Sides
Released by Geffen (Japan), June 1, 2000

Totally Confused
Halo of Gold
Burro
Brother
Lemonade
Electric Music and the Summer People
Clock
Feather in Your Cap

This Japanese-only collection gathers various B-sides and album bonus tracks into one convenient package.

Beck
Released by Interscope, February 20, 2001

Arabian Nights
Dirty Dirty
Midnite Vultures
Mixed Bizness (Latin-Shot mix by Scatter-Shot Theory)
Mixed Bizness (Hardmixn by Jake Kozel)
Salt in the Wound
Sexx Laws (Malibu Remix)
Zatyricon

Originally titled *Perpendicular Sidewalk* and available exclusively online through Beck.com, the collection includes the "Nicotine & Gravy" video as bonus CD-ROM content. The two "Mixed Bizness" remixes were provided by fans who entered a Beck.com remix contest that Beck himself judged.

SINGLES

"MTV Makes Me Want to Smoke Crack"
Released by Gusto Productions/Flipside Records, 1993

Side A (Beck):
MTV Makes Me Want to Smoke Crack
To See That Woman of Mine

Side B (Bean):
Privates on Parade
Rock > Scissors > Paper

Beck's debut 7-inch single is a split single with Bean and was issued as 1,000 pieces of clear blue vinyl. Extremely rare and virtually impossible to find. The version of "MTV Makes Me Want to Smoke Crack" found here is the little-heard original version.

"Loser"
Released by Bong Load Custom Records, 1993

Side A:
Loser

Side B:
Steal My Body Home

Beck's first Bong Load release and the reason why we know him today.

"Steve Threw Up"
Released by Bong Load Custom Records, 1993

Side A:
Steve Threw Up

Side B:
Mutherfuker
Untitled

"Steve Threw Up" was recorded by Tom Grimley at Poop Alley, while "Mutherfuker" was recorded by Tom and Rob. The A-side of the vinyl has "Time to Rock" scratched into it, while the B-side has "Smash the Clock" cryptically inscribed.

"Loser"
Released by DGC/Bong Load Custom Records, January 1994

Loser
Corvette Bummer
Alcohol
Soul Suckin Jerk (Reject)
Fume

Beck's first product on Geffen finds the label collecting together four previously unreleased B-sides, one of which is an alternate take of the album cut "Soul Suckin Jerk," as well as the album version of the A-side. An interesting note is that the jukebox 45 of "Loser" contains "Alcohol" as its B-side. The U.K. version of the single adds "Totally Confused," "Corvette Bummer," and "MTV Makes Me Want to Smoke Crack" to fill out the complement. The 7-inch in Britain was limited to 1,500 copies and included "Alcohol" and "Fume" as B-sides.

"Beercan"
Released by DGC/Bong Load Custom Records, 1994

Beercan
Got No Mind
Asskizz Powergrudge (Payback '94)
Totally Confused
Spanking Room
Loser ("Muzak version")

This was another juicy offering from Geffen to fans who were clamoring for more sweet rarities. "Got No Mind" is actually an unused take of "Pay No Mind," and there's an unlisted Muzak version of "Loser" tacked on at the end. The U.K. version of the single contains one less track than the U.S. model and is otherwise the same. The British vinyl version comes with "Spanking Room" as the B-side and was released in a run of 1,500.

"Pay No Mind (Snoozer)"
Released by Geffen/Bong Load Custom Records, 1994

Pay No Mind (Snoozer)
Special People

Trouble All My Days
Supergolden (Sunchild)

All three B-sides are taken from *Golden Feelings*. The U.K. version of this single is identical with some exceptions to the packaging. However, the U.K. 7-inch, which slaps on "Special People" as its sole B-side, was limited to 1,500 copies and is subsequently impossible to find.

"It's All in Your Mind"
Released by K Records, 1995

Side A:
It's All in Your Mind

Side B:
Feather in Your Cap
Whiskey Can Can

Songs Beck recorded with Calvin Johnson in 1993. This 7-incher is still pretty easy to come across. One pressing of the single was accidentally minted up on clear brown vinyl and is now a collector's item.

"Where It's At"
Released by Geffen/Bong Load Custom Records, June 1996

Side A:
Where It's At (Edit)
Make Out City (remix by Mike Simpson)
Where It's At (remix by Mario C. and Mickey P.)

Side B:
Where It's At (remix by John King)
Bonus Beats

The U.S. vinyl version is the first of many permutations of this single. The U.S. CD single version includes "Where It's At (Edit)," "Where It's At (remix by John King)," "Lloyd Price Express (remix by John King)," "Dark and Lovely (remix by Dust Brothers)," "American Wasteland (remix by Mickey P.)," and "Clock." The Australian and British markets chose to release it as a CD single with only the A-side, "Bonus Beats," and the Mario C. and Mickey P. remix added. In addition, the U.K. also released it on 12-inch, switching out the John King remix in favor of an U.N.K.L.E. remix. Finally, the Japanese version of the single includes some exclusive remixes as well as the hard-to-obtain track "Clock."

"Devils Haircut"
Released by Geffen/Bong Load Custom Records, November 1996

Part One:
Devils Haircut
Dark and Lovely (remix by Dust Brothers)
American Wasteland (remix by Mickey P.)
000.000

Part Two:
Devils Haircut
Devils Haircut (remix by Noel Gallagher)
Groovy Sunday (remix by Mike Simpson)
Trouble All My Days

This U.K. two-parter is rife with remixes and the previously unheard "000.000." Noel Gallagher's revved-up guitar version of the A-side was dissed endlessly by the U.K. press. The Australian take on the single included the A-side, the "Dark and Lovely" remix, and the "American Wasteland" reworking. In the U.S., the label chose to release a limited run of 2,000 7-inchers that featured John King's "Lloyd Prince Express" remix as the only B-side. It was also issued as an EP with the following B-sides, "Dark and Lovely (remix by Dust Brothers)," "American Wasteland (remix by Mickey P.)," "Lloyd Price Express (remix by John King)," and "Clock."

"The New Pollution"
Released by Geffen/Bong Load Custom Records, February 1997

Part One:
The New Pollution
The New Pollution (remix by Mario C. & Mickey P.)
Lemonade

Part Two:
The New Pollution

Electric Music and the Summer People
Richard's Hairpiece (remix by Aphex Twin)

The Australian EP release is the same as the second part of the U.K. release. The U.S. 7-inch release features "Electric Music and the Summer People" as its B-side. The U.S. EP release includes all of the tracks above and Mickey P.'s singular take on the A-side. The Japanese then expanded that tracklisting to include "Thunderpeel" from *Stereopathetic Soul Manure,* "Feather in Your Cap" from the *subUrbia* soundtrack, and "ooo.ooo," titling the effort *The New Pollution and Other Favorites.* And to appease and infuriate computer geeks and audiophiles alike, Beck issued "The New Pollution" as a European single with the Mickey P. remix as a B-side and the videos for "Where It's At" and "The New Pollution" as CD-ROM extra bonus material.

"Sissyneck"
Released by Geffen/Bong Load Custom Records, 1997

Sissyneck
Burro (Mariachi version of Jack-Ass)
Dark and Lovely (remix by Dust Brothers)
Devil Got My Woman
Brother

This Australian tour EP also came banded to various pressings of *Odelay*. The Brits chose to slap on "Feather in Your Cap" as well as Mickey P.'s remix of "The New Pollution." The U.S. 7-inch release saw "Feather in Your Cap" used as a B-side and pressed up in an edition of 1,500.

"Jack-Ass"
Released by Geffen/Bong Load Custom Records, August 1997

Jack-Ass (Butch Vig Mix)
Jack-Ass (Lowrider Mix by Butch Vig)
Burro
Strange Invitation
Devil Got My Woman
Brother

"Burro" is a mariachi take of "Jack-Ass," while "Strange Invitation" is an orchestral version of "Jack-Ass," and "Devil Got My Woman" is a cover of the Skip James tune.

The U.S. 7-inch pressing has the same tracklisting, though the CD EP features only Butch Vig's mix, "Burro," "Strange Invitation," and "Brother." However, as usual, the Germans mix it up entirely by putting on their EP the album version of the A-side, the Butch Vig mix, "Feather in Your Cap," and "Lemonade."

"Deadweight"
Released by Geffen, October 27, 1997

Deadweight (edit)
Erase the Sun
SA-5

Taken from the *A Life Less Ordinary* soundtrack, the U.K. and Australian versions slap on two throwaway B-sides, while the 7-inch version only includes "Erase the Sun."

"Tropicalia"
Released by Geffen/Bong Load Custom Records, November 3, 1998

Tropicalia
Halo of Gold
Black Balloon

"Halo of Gold" is from the *More Oar* tribute album. The U.K. 7-incher has only "Halo of Gold" as a B-side and was released in a run of 1,500.

"Nobody's Fault But My Own"
Released by Geffen/Bong Load Custom Records, April 1999

Nobody's Fault But My Own
One of These Days
Diamond in the Sleaze

This Japanese-only pressing came out to coincide with Beck's *Mutations* tour of Japan and included two new B-sides.

"Cold Brains"
Released by Geffen/Bong Load Custom Records, spring 1999

Cold Brains
Electric Music and the Summer People

Halo of Gold
Runners Dial Zero
Diamond Bollocks

This promo-only single was released to U.S. stations in the spring of 1999 to keep Beck in the minds of radio programmers while he worked on *Midnite Vultures*.

"Sexx Laws"
Released by Geffen, October 25, 1999

Part One:
Sexx Laws
This Is My Crew
Sexx Laws (WIseguys Remix)

Part Two:
Sexx Laws
Salt in the Wound
Sexx Laws (Malibu Mix by Roger Manning)

This U.K. two-parter comes with two remixes and two new B-sides for eager Beck fanatics. Through beckdirect.com in the States, fans could purchase one of 1,000 clear 12-inch versions of the single that came with the Roger Manning mix as a B-side. The U.K. also released a 7-inch picture disc with "Salt in the Wound" as a B-side.

"Mixed Bizness"
Released by Geffen, March 27, 2000

Part One:
Mixed Bizness
Mixed Bizness (Nu Wave Dreamix by Les Rythmes Digitales)
Dirty Dirty

Part Two:
Mixed Bizness
Mixed Bizness (Cornelius Remix)
Mixed Bizness (DJ Me DJ You Remix)

Part Two of the single also includes a CD-ROM bonus of the "Mixed Bizness" video.

The U.S. EP version of this includes all of the above-listed tracks, as well as the "Sexx Laws" permutation "Saxx Laws (Night Flight to Ojai)." The U.S. 12-inch version mixes it up by offering the very eighties Les Rythmes Digitales remix, the Cornelius remix, a new remix by Bix Pender, and "Dirty Dirty" as B-sides. Once again, the Germans feel an uncontrollable urge to be different, so they commission a version of the single with the Les Rythmes Digitales remix, "Dirty Dirty," and "Die Fanastischen Vier (Transatlantik Remix)," those wacky bastards. In addition, the European single features the Bix Pender remix, the Les Rythmes Digitales take, and the previously unheard "Arabian Nights."

"Nicotine & Gravy"
Released by Geffen, July 30, 2000

Nicotine & Gravy
Midnite Vultures
Zatyricon

This European single comes with two unheard tracks from the *Midnite Vultures* sessions, as well as the CD-ROM bonus of the little-seen "Nicotine & Gravy" video.

REMIXES

Jon Spencer Blues Explosion, *Experimental Remixes*
Released by Matador, 1995

Beck, along with his esteemed associates Mike D. of the Beasties and Mario Caldato Jr., remixes "Flavor."

Air, "Sexy Boy" single
Released by Caroline, 1998

Beck remixes the French duo's ubiquitous club hit and entitles it "Sex Kino mix."

Air, "Kelly Watch the Stars" single
Released by Caroline, 1998

Includes the same remix of "Sexy Boy" as heard on the "Sexy Boy" single.

Björk, "Hunter" single
Released by Elektra, 1998

This French release features the "Bjeck Remix" of Björk's "Alarm Call" from her *Homogenic* album.

David Bowie, "Seven" single Pt. 1
Released by Virgin, July 2000

This U.K. single finds Beck remixing the Thin White Duke's "Seven" from *hours . . .* and adding a touch of Roger Manning Jr.'s acoustic piano to the new mix.

COLLABORATIONS AND APPEARANCES

Black Fag, *Parerga y Paralipomena* EP
Released by Amoeba Records & Filmworks, 1992

Beck is credited with production of this 7-inch EP

The Geraldine Fibbers, *Get Thee Gone*
Released by Sympathy for the Record Industry, 1994

Beck cowrote the tune "Blue Cross" and appears on the track alongside Presidents of the United States of America frontman Chris Ballew.

Jon Spencer Blues Explosion, *Orange*
Released by Matador, 1994

Beck appears as a rapper extraordinaire on the track "Flavor."

Caspar and Mollusk, *Twig* EP
Released by Cosmic Records, 1995

This collaboration with Chris Ballew finds Beck working his magic on the A-side.

Black Fag, "Harrow House"
Released by Amoeba Records & Filmworks, 1995

Beck produced this 12-incher.

Various Artists, *The Poop Alley Tapes*
Released by Win Records, 1996

Beck and the kids of that dog redo "Girl Dreams," which originally appeared on *One Foot in the Grave*.

Forest for the Trees, *Forest for the Trees*
Released by Dreamworks, 1997

Carl Stephenson's side project finds Beck providing backing vocals on "Infinite Cow" and harmonica on "Fall."

Various Artists, *Hear You Me!*
Released by Vast Records, January 27, 1998

On this tribute to the Weezer fans Mykel and Carli killed in a car accident, Beck contributes his formidable banjo skills on that dog track "Silently."

Amnesia, *Lingus*
Released by Supreme/Island Records, July 14, 1998

Beck lays down some harmonica on "Drop Down." Also of interest is that Beck's dad, David Campbell, does string arrangements for "Swimming Lessons," "Train Try," and "Leaving," while Justin Meldal-Johnson gives some bass to "The Sensual Corgi."

Kahimi Karie, *Kahimi Karie*
Released by Minty Fresh, September 8, 1998

On "Lolitapop Dollhouse" you'll hear Mr. Hansen noodling on the harmonica.

Various Artists, *The Rugrats Movie Soundtrack*
Released by Interscope Records, November 3, 1998

Along with the likes of Iggy Pop, Jakob Dylan of the Wallflowers, Laurie Anderson, B-Real of Cypress Hill, Phife of A Tribe Called Quest, and Lenny Kravitz, Beck sings two lines in "This World Is Something New to Me."

Various Artists, *The Hi-Lo Country Soundtrack*
Released by TVT Soundtrax, January 19, 1999

Willie Nelson and Beck duet for the classic Floyd Tillman tune "Drivin' Nails in my Coffin."

Forest for the Trees, *The Sound of Wet Paint* EP
Released by Dreamworks, March 9, 1999

Beck's work is randomly heard in the midst of "Jet Engine."

Various Artists, *Farm Aid Volume One*
Released by Redline Entertainment, September 12, 2000

Beck and Willie Nelson's rendition of Jimmie Rodgers's country classic "Peach Pickin' Time In Georgia" from their 1997 Farm Aid appearance is included here.

COMPILATIONS
(There are numerous instances when an album version of a song has been used for a movie soundtrack or collection. These instances have been omitted here for the sake of the author's already questionable sanity.)

Various Artists, *Rare on Air: Live Performances Volume 1*
Released by Mammoth, 1994

Beck's live version from KCRW of "Mexico" is included here.

Various Artists, *DGC Rarities Volume 1*
Released by DGC Records, 1994

Beck contributes his pisstake of Pearl Jam's "Even Flow," entitled "Bogusflow."

Various Artists, *KXLU Live Volume One*
Released by KXLU, 1995

Beck donates "Whiskey-Faced," "Radioactive," and "Blowdryin' Lady" from his KXLU sessions.

Various Artists, *Periscope: Another Yo Yo Compilation*
Released by Yo Yo, 1995

Beck contributes "The World May Loose Its Motion" from the Poop Alley sessions.

Various Artists, *Skookum Chief Powered Teenage Zit Rock Angst Presented by Nardwuar the Human Serviette*
Released by Nardwuar the Human Serviette, 1995

A phone conversation taped between Nardwuar (who quickly fell out of graces with all and sundry for his telepranks) and Beck.

Various Artists, *Yo Yo a Go Go*
Released by Yo Yo, 1996

This collection highlights selected tracks taken from 1995's Yo Yo a Go Go festival up in Olympia, Washington. Beck's performance is immortalized here with one untitled track and a rendition of "Sleeping Bag."

Various Artists, *Just Say Noel*
Released by Geffen, 1996

Beck's now perennial favorite "Little Drum Machine Boy" is captured here with a bevy of other holiday tunes.

Various Artists, *KXLU Demolisten Volume 2*
Released by No Life Records, 1996

Beck gives away another untitled live composition.

Various Artists, *Kill the Moonlight* soundtrack
Released by Sympathy for the Record Industry, 1997

Beck donates "Leave Me on the Moon," "I Sold My Souls Innermost for Some Pickled Fish," and "Underwater Music" to the soundtrack of Steve Hanft's movie.

Various Artists, *A Life Less Ordinary* soundtrack
Released by A&M Records, 1997

Alongside luminaries such as R.E.M., Ash, Prodigy, and Folk Implosion, Beck contributes "Deadweight."

Various Artists, subUrbia soundtrack
Released by DGC, 1997

This version of "Feather In Your Cap" differs from the "All in Your Mind" 7-inch version, as it was recorded in 1994 with Tom Rothrock and Rob Schnapf.

Various Artists, WBCN Naked Disc
Released by Wicked Disc, 1997

Another live contribution as Beck donates "One Foot in the Grave (Live at Fort Apache Studios 8/9/97)" to the collection.

Various Artists, Tibetan Freedom Concert
Released by Grand Royal/Capitol, 1997

Peers such as Radiohead, U2, Foo Fighters, and Sonic Youth dot the sleeve to this massive collection that includes Beck's awesome rendition of "Asshole."

Various Artists, Bridge School Concert Volume 1
Released by Reprise, November 11, 1997

Beck's 1995 performance of "It's All in Your Mind" makes the cut.

Various Artists, Selector Dub Narcotic
Released by K Records, 1998

Recorded around 1993 or 1994, "Close to God" was worked up under the watchful eye of Calvin Johnson.

Various Artists, More Oar: A Tribute to Alexander "Skip" Spence
Released by Birdman Records, July 6, 1999

A touching cover of "Halo of Gold" appears courtesy of Beck.

Various Artists, Return of the Grievous Angel: A Tribute to Gram Parsons
Released by Almo Sounds, July 13, 1999

Duetting with Emmylou Harris, Beck moans out "Sin City."

Various Artists, *SNL 25: Saturday Night Live Musical Performance Volume 2*
Released by Dreamworks, September 21, 1999

Here you'll find Beck's January 9, 1999, performance of "Nobody's Fault But My Own."

Various Artists, *At Home With the Groovebox*
Released by Grand Royal, March 2000

Beck contributes the groovalicious "Boyz."

Various Artists, *A Hot Wild Drive in the City*
Released by Gusto Productions, 2000

This rerelease offers up the ancient Beck track "Put It in Neutral," as well as the track "American Car" by the Steve Moramarco-helmed Bean, with Beck on backing vox. This second track can also be found on a limited-edition flexidisc with the May/June 2000 issue of *Glue* magazine.

Various Artists, *Sounds Eclectic*
Released on April 3, 2001

Beck's live cover of Hank Williams and Jimmie Davis's "(I Heard That) Lonesome Whistle Blow" from a KCRW *Morning Becomes Eclectic* performance is included here.

Various Artists, *Moulin Rouge* soundtrack
Released by Interscope Records, May 8, 2001

Beck covers David Bowie's "Diamond Dogs" for this Baz Luhrman flick.

"Loser" directed by Steve Hanft

"Beercan" directed by Steve Hanft

"Pay No Mind" directed by Steve Hanft

"Forcefield" directed by Patrick Maley

"Where It's At" directed by Steve Hanft

"Devils Haircut" directed by Mark Romanek

"The New Pollution" directed by Beck Hansen

"Jack-Ass" directed by Steve Hanft

"Deadweight" directed by Michael Gondry

"Sexx Laws" directed by Beck Hansen

Note: There also exists an "Extended" version and an "Escape to Ojai Mix" of the video, both of which include extra footage and were overseen by Beck himself.

"Mixed Bizness" directed by Stephane Sednaoui

"Nicotine & Gravy" directed by Fullerene Productions

Note: This video was only released in Europe.

"Flavor" Jon Spencer Blues Explosion directed by Evan Bernard

Note: Beck plays a variety of roles (chef, DJ, toy salesman, and lounge singer) alongside Beastie Boy Mike D. in this clip for his remix of the JSBE song.

"Love Spreads" Stone Roses directed by Steve Hanft

Note: Beck plays a gold panner in a brief cameo.

PHOTO COURTESY OF SCOTT GRIES/IMAGE DIRECT

www.beck.com Beck.com—The official site and overflowing with news, a killer discography, multimedia goodies, and his online store. What more could Bekkies ask for?

http://slojamcentral.tripod.com Beck @ Slo-Jam Central—Hands down the best unofficial Beck site with great up-to-date news, show reviews, pictures, and much more.

http://www.soreeyesimaging.com/beck/homepage.asp—Biscuits & Bacon on Beck—Beautifully designed and full o' stuff, this is one of the best Beck websites out there.

http://www.geocities.com/SunsetStrip/Club/5444/beck.html Planet Beck—Land here for a Beck chat room, some cool downloads (Beck icons for the internet generation), and adulation galore for the artist known solely as Beck.

http://www.freespeech.org/pacey/ Beck! Beck! Beck!—A loving tribute to the man himself.

http://www.freespeech.org/beck_fishbulb/ Beck: Enchanting Wizard of Rhythm—Beck-inspired poetry and artwork as well as a three-level trivia quiz and plenty of info. One-stop shopping for the obsessed.

http://www.chez.com/cyanidebeckmint/index.html Cyanide Beck Mint—It's in French, but it's cool.

http://faisons.com/beck/tab.html Somabottle's Beck Tabs—So you wanna be like the man? Well then pick up yer guitar and strum along to the contents of this website.

http://www.geocities.com/SunsetStrip/towers/9782/beck.html Beck! The Setlists—Over a hundred shows lovingly mapped out for the curious Beck fan.